'I highly commend this refresh[ing] [way] which Derek Williams uses Jud[as], [the] icon of betrayal, to challenge us [to] [see] ourselves and more generous[ly] [...] Williams' accessible style, richly combining Christian reflection with telling historical and contemporary references, provides a realistic yet encouraging view of humanity, leading us to more gracious living.'
The Venerable Richard Brand, Archdeacon of Winchester

'Here is practical wisdom on how to protect against our inbuilt tendency to go wrong. Derek Williams is readable, thoughtful, brave, startling, challenging, encouraging: take this book seriously, and you will grow as a disciple of Jesus Christ. I recommend it highly.'
Donald Allister, Bishop of Peterborough

The Judas Trap

Why people mess up
(and how to avoid joining them)

Derek Williams

Derek Williams

instant
ap stle

First published in Great Britain in 2016.

Instant Apostle
The Barn
1 Watford House Lane
Watford
Herts
WD17 1BJ

British Library Cataloguing-in-Publication Data

A catalogue record for this book is available from the British Library

This book and all other Instant Apostle books are available from Instant Apostle:

Website: www.instantapostle.com
E-mail: info@instantapostle.com

ISBN 978-1-909728-54-7

Printed in Great Britain

Contents

Foreword

The Judas Trap is a fascinating challenge to us all. We are encouraged to seek to understand what might have made Judas Iscariot deliver Jesus Christ to the Roman authorities, as described in the New Testament. Judas is a very important person in the story of Jesus for Christians, as he is considered to have 'betrayed' Jesus. Judas is the person who started the process of Jesus' crucifixion. So it is important to face the possibility that any one of us may have done exactly the same, had we found ourselves where Judas was.

Derek Williams gives us clear, possible explanations for why Judas did what he did, all backed by referenced evidence from the literature and lots of easy-to-read examples, both historical and contemporary. He has done a thorough job of investigating his topic of *The Judas Trap*. Maybe the reasons Judas did what he did can apply to all of us. We are encouraged to think how we might be at risk of falling into one of the same traps, even 2,000 years later.

The explanations use theories from many disciplines: psychology, sociology, economics, ethics and more. Derek uses the evidence well to support his proposed possible explanations of Judas' behaviour. Each chapter addresses a single possible explanation, starting with a clear, brief summary of what is in the chapter (what an invaluable aspect of this book), an apposite quotation, a description of the 'trap' factor to be discussed, then the evidence and anecdote.

But there is more. Each chapter then challenges the reader as to whether we may fall into this specific trap, and then gives practical suggestions on what we can do to avoid doing that. Perfect! We are led through the process of thinking how awful it would have been for Judas to do that; how, maybe, there was a reason why he did it; well, maybe, we sometimes behave a bit like that, too; but here's how we can avoid doing it any more. Phew!

This book challenges the reader to think. It is easy to read, well signposted and very engaging. You may want to pause between each chapter to think. I suggest your thinking will be interesting. You will have been charmingly, gently challenged. Do accept the challenge and see where this excellent book takes you.

Dr Hilary Hearnshaw
Associate Professor Emeritus of Primary Care, University of Warwick

Introduction: People can be so unpredictable!

'What went on in that head of his? ... Other lives were housed in that mind, parallel worlds. Maybe we're all built a little bit that way.'[1]

We live in an amazing world. Compared to the vastness of the universe – billions of stars, countless planets stretching into infinity – it is 'a mote of dust suspended in a sunbeam,' to use the words of astrophysicist Carl Sagan.[2]

Yet its complex and finely balanced structure, still being sculpted by the huge forces of volcanic fire, tempestuous water, roaring wind and quaking earth, is teeming with a huge variety of life. There are some 950,000 species of insects, 400,000 known species of plants, 10,500 species of birds and some 4,000 species of mammals. Take a walk in a park or the countryside sometime, notice the variety and complexity of life that is all around you, and be amazed.

One of those 4,000 mammals, *homo sapiens*, human beings, has itself created a hugely complex substructure of civilisation. We have harnessed many of the natural resources of the earth (processing some to create new materials) and from them built physical wonders, from skyscrapers to satellite communications. We have learned to harvest the earth to create a wide range of foods. We have invented colourful cultures, enduring customs; we have developed varied structures of government and commerce.

Look around your home or working environment. Notice the electrical equipment, invented, designed and manufactured from many different resources by many different people. Notice how it is quietly humming with power cabled in from goodness knows where, the supply generated and maintained from more natural resources by more anonymous people. Everything around you is an invention and creation of ingenious human beings who have sought to improve life for all of us.

Think, too, of the great achievements of art and architecture, sport and science, of acts of heroism and daring exploration. Remember the universal human qualities of sensitive care and love for young and old exhibited in ordinary family life and in the extraordinary dedication of specialists working with the emergency services to save the lives of strangers. Think of fun and enjoyment, laughter and leisure. Think of all these things, and be amazed.

We really do live in an amazing world. But sometimes things go wrong.

People don't behave as we expect them to. Some do bad things to each other. This delicate world of beauty and wonder is also a world where war and violence rage. The fragile network of human cooperation and creativity can become a tangled web of hate, greed and aggression. All ordinary, decent people are, at some points in our lives, inconsiderate, selfish and insensitive. Human beings are not perfect.

We all make mistakes. We do or say things that we later regret. To err is human, and with the best will in the world, we can never be absolutely sure what we will do in any combination of circumstances. And we are highly prone to putting a glossy spin on our own shortcomings compared with the disapproval we mete out to others. Based on the results of experiments which test human codes of behaviour, social psychologist Cordelia Fine suggests that 'People's moral stamina is but a leaf blown hither and thither by the winds of circumstance.'[3]

Of course, we don't usually want to ruin things for ourselves or for others, although there may be occasions when we do strike out wilfully. Often we never intend to mess up: it just kind of happens. And we look back and think, why did I do that? What possessed me? We struggle, as St Paul did, with sometimes failing to do the good things we should do, or by doing things which are not in our or other people's best interests.[4]

Why? Why, when there is so much potential for good do we sink into an abyss of mediocrity or worse? What triggers such lapses; how can we avoid them and help others to do the same? How should we feel about and deal with people who fall, wilfully or accidentally, from grace? That is what this book explores. By considering such matters, we shall be in a stronger position to reinforce the good and restrict the bad, in ourselves and in others.

But all the while we do so, there is one important thing to remember. Despite all the lapses, this world, and the people in it, are still amazing. If you base your view of humanity only on the headlines in news bulletins, you might assume that the world is thoroughly rotten. But news in the modern world is by definition that which is an exception. Picnics in the park are not news. Riots in the park are. But the picnics are far more frequent than the riots. Our task is to recover our amazement, and to strengthen our resolve to cherish it.

We take as our starting point one person whose dramatic failure of judgement has become a household name. Step back some 2,000 years for a moment.

The kiss of Judas

Jesus had just forecast that someone in his trusted circle of 12 apostles would betray him and that the others would run away scared. Peter, the motormouth of the group, asserted that even if they did, he wouldn't. So when Jesus went on to predict Peter's own fall from grace the apostle declared, '"Even if I have to die with you, I will never disown you." And all the other disciples said the same.'

But when push came to shove, they all did just as Jesus had predicted. Judas Iscariot revealed Jesus' whereabouts to the authorities so that they could arrest him. In a dark and secluded olive grove where Jesus had gone to pray, illuminated only by the flickering light of flaming torches carried by a group of soldiers, Judas identified Jesus in the gloom by giving him that now infamous kiss.

Shortly afterwards, Peter openly denied ever having known Jesus. The others ran and hid in fear for their own lives. Jesus was left alone in the world, at the mercy of people intent on silencing his potentially revolutionary gospel of peace.[5]

Over the centuries a number of factors have been identified as possible causes of Judas Iscariot's otherwise inexplicable act of betraying Jesus. The most likely scenario is that there was no single reason. A combination of several factors created the perfect storm in Judas' mind. It is often the sheer complexity of nurture and nature, of circumstance and choice, that makes us the people we are and drives our actions and our attitudes for better or worse.

However, I am not offering a detailed examination of Judas' life. There are a number of deeper studies on that topic, not least Peter Stanford's recent excellent survey, *Judas: The Troubling History of the Renegade Apostle*.[6] Rather, I am summarising the basic information and using it as a springboard, an illustrative case, of the issues Judas raises. From him we move on to draw insights and lessons from many fields and stories from different times.

The factors in Judas' life which may have contributed to his lapse are common and timeless. By examining them we can discover how to avoid making similar mistakes, how we might turn our potential weaknesses into strengths, and thus improve our lives and make our world a better place. We may also find fresh, more creative ways of thinking about, and reacting to, people around us who let us or themselves down, in a way that perhaps brokers some healing or prevents wrongs from being multiplied.

In the course of it we shall use material from the Christian Bible. (To avoid cluttering the text all references are collected in endnotes at the end of each chapter.) Despite its vintage and its complexity, the Bible is an astonishingly rich source of wisdom and practical advice about human life in all its dimensions. That is perhaps not so surprising if you recall that Jesus said that his mission was to endow people with life, and that 'they may ... have it to the full'.[7]

You don't need to be a Bible scholar to read this book. You just need to be a human being interested in the development and improvement of the whole person and our wonderful – but also frustrating – world. Just think what our lives, and our world, might be like if we could reduce such factors as hatred, discord, envy, greed, abuse of power, selfish ambition, blind bigotry and desperate despair – things that can make our own and other people's lives a misery. And think how much better things would be if there was a greater torrent of love, joy, peace, forbearance, kindness, goodness, faithfulness, gentleness and self-control flowing through the world.[8]

Some 700 years before Christ a wise prophet said this: 'What does the Lord require of you? To act justly and to love mercy and to walk humbly with your God.'[9] Justice, mercy and humility: those three traits will be our anchor as we venture into the turbulent waters of human weakness and failure.

It is no good leaving that journey to others. It has to begin with us. And the best place to start is to discover just how 'normal' Judas was, exactly as many other notorious people were, or seemed to be. Let's meet some.

Notes

[1] From the novel by Karen Thompson Walker, *The Age of Miracles*, Simon & Schuster, 2012, p.118.
[2] Carl Sagan quoted in *The Times*, 24 July 2013.
[3] Cordelia Fine, *A Mind of its Own*, Icon Books, 2007, p.71.
[4] See St Paul's anguished confession in Romans 7:18-25.
[5] Matthew 26:31-56, 69-75.
[6] Peter Stanford, *Judas: The Troubling History of the Renegade Apostle*, Hodder & Stoughton, 2015.
[7] John 10:10.
[8] Galatians 5:22-23.
[9] Micah 6:8.

Chapter 1
He was just like one of us

Some people who mess up – Judas included – start out as surprisingly 'normal'. Decent, ordinary people sometimes do outrageous, or 'out of character', things. Being aware of the pressures can help us to understand them and avoid following their example.

The line dividing good and evil cuts through the heart of every human being. During the life of any heart this keeps changing place; sometimes it is squeezed one way by exuberant evil and sometimes it shifts to allow space for good to flourish. One and the same human being is, at various ages, under various circumstances, a totally different human being. At times he is close to being a devil, at times to sainthood. But his name doesn't change, and to that name we ascribe the whole lot, good and evil.[1]

We all like to think that we are 'normal', 'ordinary', 'decent' people. There is a problem with this. We are all different; we have different personalities, backgrounds, knowledge and experience. My idea of 'normal' or 'ordinary' isn't quite the same as yours. We easily underestimate our differences. Not everyone can do or achieve what you do or have achieved, and not everyone thinks or feels as you do. They may have different standards of behaviour or different beliefs which we can debate, even decry, but to them they are 'normal'.

Most of us, though (apart from people who for various reasons actively seek publicity), don't want to be *so* different that we risk attracting headlines or being thought odd. Our general idea of an ordinary decent person is one who just gets on with life, who provides for his or her family; who doesn't break the law; who helps others out when necessary; who talks about everyday things: the weather, the sports results, the goods and prices in the shops; who isn't extreme in their opinions or bizarre in their actions.

And that probably accounts for about 98 per cent of all the people we shall ever rub shoulders with. None of us is perfect, of course. I'm just as likely to fail to meet my own standards of behaviour as anyone else is. Although, if I'm honest, I'm more likely to find a plausible excuse for my errors than I am to overlook or forgive easily those of others.

So we are often taken aback when someone in the public eye, or someone we know, apparently messes up big time. We might even dismiss the idea that they have done so at first: there must be some mistake; she's such a nice person; he'd never hurt a fly.

Before we look in later chapters at some specific triggers that may launch people into disastrous trajectories, let us first identify four kinds of 'normal' person whose actions depart from what is expected or regarded as normal and decent. The examples may in some cases surprise you. Just as the actions of our anti-hero, Judas Iscariot, surprised the first Christians.

Judas the apostle

If ever there was a normal person in a team, it was Judas Iscariot. He never aroused suspicion. There is only one sour note in the entire gospel record, and even that is written in retrospect: John's terse claim that Judas, the group treasurer, cooked the books.[2] Indeed, John confirms that there were no early signs of Judas' double dealing. In his list of the apostles, he refers to Judas as 'one of the Twelve [who] was *later* to betray him'.[3] Luke implies the same in his list: 'Judas Iscariot, who *became* a traitor' – that is, well after being called by Jesus.[4]

So when Jesus sent out the 12 in pairs to preach, teach, heal and cast out demons, Judas was among them. Any deviation on his part would have been noted. He was neither excused the task by Jesus nor did he exempt himself from it. He must have exhibited the same spiritual power and authority as the others.

We can only assume that Judas was as excited and effective as the others were, and that he was well integrated into the band of apostles.[5] He was a normal human being, with his own strengths and weaknesses. He had the same potential for success and failure as any one of us. For a while, he may even have done a very good job.

The nineteenth-century Baptist preacher Charles Haddon Spurgeon put this graphically:

> You might not have known, by mere sight, which was the better man of the two – John or Judas. Most probably you would have preferred the gentle manners of John; but I would suppose – for our Lord never chose a man to an office unless he had some qualification – you would have admired the calm prudence of Judas, and his quiet business tact … They sat at the same table, engaged in the same exercises, and looked much the same kind of men. None of us would have guessed that one of them

was John the divine, and the other was Judas the devil.[6]

Christians sometimes struggle to reconcile Judas' genuine spiritual ministry with his later rejection of Jesus. Some suggest that he wasn't truly committed. That is based on one comment in which Jesus is said to have known in advance people who 'did not believe and who would betray him'.[7] But this is tenuous for three reasons. One is that linguistically Jesus is referring to separate groups. Another is that none of the 12 truly 'believed' until after Jesus' resurrection, despite occasional outbursts of faith such as Peter's declaration that Jesus was the Christ (Messiah).[8]

And the third is that in such a close band of men pursued by jealous authorities, any hint of deviation would have been immediately attacked, and there is no record of anything like that happening. The remaining 11 must have been as puzzled as we are by Judas' final actions.

Besides, there are numerous other biblical accounts of human inconsistency. For example, when Jesus rebuked one of the disciples as a stumbling block who knew nothing of the ways of God, it wasn't Judas he was talking to. It was Peter, the group spokesman and future leader of the church, who was told to 'Get behind me, Satan!'[9]

Later in the New Testament Paul writes of people who have rejected Christian teachings and practices 'and so have suffered shipwreck with regard to the faith'.[10] The implication is that they were well on course until they hit the rocks for reasons he doesn't explain. The author of the letter to the Hebrews urges his readers to keep the faith so that they don't fail to enter God's 'rest'.[11]

The Old Testament is positively tabloid in its exposure of pillars of faith who soiled their own reputations: King David's adultery with Bathsheba (which involved the arranged murder of her husband) being one of the most famous.[12] David, of course, went on to maintain his reputation as the ancient Israelites' greatest king, and the revered ancestor of the promised Messiah.[13]

In other words, people who start well but fall on the way are more common than we imagine. They don't signal their decline and fall in advance. They probably don't even imagine themselves capable of falling – neither do most of us – and they carry on normally afterwards.

So to the first of our four types of normal but erring person: the one whose errors are more of omission than commission.

Type 1: the preoccupied person

Jesus' story of the Good Samaritan is etched into many people's consciousness. A traveller – probably a merchant – was attacked by thieves on a lonely road, and left for dead. Two religious professionals came along, saw him, crossed over and passed by. Maybe they were late. Maybe their scruples balked at the risk of becoming ceremonially unclean if the man was dead and they were to touch him.

Then a Samaritan, object of ethnic and religious hatred by the majority of the population to which the victim belonged, stopped, administered first aid, transported the victim to a place of safety and – this being a time when no free health service existed – paid for the victim's upkeep until he recovered.[14]

My local newspaper often carries letters of appreciation from people whose lost purse has been returned by a 'good Samaritan', or who have been helped by a total stranger when they fell in the street. It's the sort of thing that Street Pastors do in many towns and cities on Friday and Saturday nights, offering water, flip-flops, a helping hand and a listening ear to drunk or distressed people.

We like to think that someone would offer us that kind of help if we ever needed it. And we probably hope that we would be that good Samaritan if circumstances required it. Do as you would be done by, and all that. It's what normal, decent people do, right? Wrong. At least, partly wrong. And there's research to prove it.

In the Good Samaritan Experiment, two American researchers, J. M. Darley and C. E. Batson, took a group of divinity students – would-be clergy and theologians – and divided them into two groups. They were told that shortly they would have to give an impromptu talk in another building on campus. Half were to talk about the value of their course to a non-ministerial career, and half were to talk about the parable of the good Samaritan.

Darley and Batson then injected some urgency into the situation. Each student was told they were either late, just about on time, or had a few extra minutes to get from A to B. As each student took the short journey, they encountered someone (who, unknown to them, was an actor) slumped and groaning by a wall.

Those who were 'late' didn't stop; nor did those who had 'just enough time'. Generally, those who had 'a few extra minutes' did stop. And it didn't matter if the students were about to deliver a talk about the Samaritan or the seminary: not even the preachers stopped to practise the moral of the story they were about to expound.[15]

The hard fact is that however much we say we care about others and are always ready to help them, we tend to do first what is most important *to us* at the time. Other people come second. It's basic self-interest. We leave the problems to someone else.

Type 2: The pressured person

If you saw someone on the edge of the top floor of a multi-storey car park, what would you do? Generally it's best to leave the emergency services to deal with it, and move on. But when Ian Lam was in such a position in Telford, Shropshire, a crowd gathered and watched. Some people who were in a hurry berated the police for barring their access to the adjoining shopping centre: preoccupation with their own concerns overcame any sense of compassion.

Others, however, urged him to jump. He did, and fell to his death. Thousands signed a petition urging the police to take action against those who apparently incited his plunge.[16] Normal people can behave badly and insensitively when a crowd mentality takes over. It pressurises us to conform.

Peer pressure can often send people off the rails. We want to be accepted by the group or remain in favour with the dominant leader. We find it hard to oppose actions, challenge assumptions or withdraw. 'Bad company corrupts good morals' is a common enough saying, the truth of which is often born out in practice. (It is in fact an observation by the Greek poet Menander, quoted with approval by St Paul.[17])

Sometimes the pressure is overwhelming, even irresistible, when accompanied by threats or sanctions against non-conformists. People feel trapped and unable to escape, however reluctant they are to do what they are told yet believe is wrong. Four classic examples illustrate this difficulty.

Reluctant soldiers

In 1942 about 500 men from the German city of Hamburg were conscripted into the Reserve Police Battalion 101. Their average age was 39, too old for front-line war duties. Most of them had never fired a shot in anger or come under enemy fire. Two-thirds of them were blue-collar workers – dockers, drivers, construction workers, machine and warehouse operatives, seamen and waiters. One-third were middle-ranking white-collar workers, mostly salesmen and office workers, with a handful of professionals such as pharmacists and teachers.

They were led to believe that they would be on guard duty. However, it soon transpired that their main job in Hitler's Order Police was to oversee the rounding up and deportation of Jews from communities in Poland, a country most of them had never previously visited. People who were too frail to be transported – the elderly, the sick and infants – were to be shot on sight.

Often the railhead was reached only after long route marches during which no food or water was provided for the Jewish prisoners. Those who collapsed along the way were shot. Those who survived were packed like sardines into sealed trucks: 150–200 people per truck with nowhere to sit, no toilet, no ventilation and no water.

Worse was to come. On one occasion, Jews were forced to dig trenches in the woods and then lie naked in them while they were sprayed with bullets. Not all were killed outright, but were smothered by the next layer of human bodies forced to lie on top of them. By the end of the war, the battalion was responsible for directly killing some 38,000 Jews and knowingly sending to death camps some 45,000 more.

The perpetrators of this crime were ordinary family men, and few had strong political beliefs or personal animosity towards the Jewish race. Their commander even gave them the chance to opt out of the gruesome task (which he himself didn't relish), but only a few did. Some were unable to carry on after they had killed a few Jews, and asked for transfers to other duties.

Christopher Browning, who chronicled this appalling chapter in wartime history, notes that 'Once the killing began, however, the men became increasingly brutalised.' During the decade-long (1962–1972) official investigation into 210 men from the battalion, some seemed to be in denial or so traumatised by what they had done that they had blotted out the memories. They had returned to normal life in which violence played no significant part.[18]

How does that happen? They simply saw no way out, and feared what might happen to them if they were to refuse their orders. Fear of reprisals, fear of ostracism, is a powerful driver. But sometimes, when a person is put into a situation of power, an almost demonic force can take over.

The Stanford Prison Experiment

Philip Zimbardo, a social psychologist, devised this famous experiment in 1971. He published the results in academic papers at the time; later it was turned into a film, and he published the full inside story for non-specialist readers.[19] From a wide pool of volunteers he chose a small group of students who were rigorously tested to ensure that they were emotionally and psychologically well balanced.

He divided them randomly into prisoners and guards and put them in a mock-up prison on campus to watch how they behaved. The guards were given some basic rules – physical violence was forbidden – but they were instructed to create a realistic atmosphere of fear and frustration. Within 24 hours some of the guards had so entered into their roles that they were making life hell for the prisoners. They woke them at all hours, and punished them for minor infringements of the rules (which they made up as they went along) with tortuous physical exercises or food deprivation. If one prisoner stepped out of line, all were punished. Soon some guards began exhibiting real excesses, including forcing the prisoners to simulate homosexual acts.

One of the guards, Chuck Burdan, had described himself as a pacifist and a non-aggressive person. Yet on the second day he was already planning ways to irritate the prisoners. On day three the sadism of some of his fellow guards annoyed him. But by day five he himself singled out one prisoner (who had gone on hunger strike) for special abuse. The pacifist had become a torturer in less than a week.

Meanwhile, the moderate guards turned blind eyes to the excesses while some prisoners' mental conditions deteriorated to breaking point. Things got so bad that the intended two-week experiment was stopped after just six days. But although it was an artificial situation, it accurately reflected real life – as Zimbardo, and the world, found out at the start of the twenty-first century.

The Abu Ghraib atrocities

In October 2003, United States Staff Sergeant Chip Frederick was put in charge of some 400 prisoners in Abu Ghraib prison in Baghdad, Iraq. Before long he was participating in the physical abuse, torture and humiliation which was routinely meted out to the detainees. The abuse is most remembered for the widely published photograph of Specialist Lyndie England holding a naked Iraqi male on a dog leash.

Yet afterwards some of the torturers found their own actions inexplicable. Something had made them change temporarily. Frederick was the most senior of a number of army personnel later convicted in the courts for their crimes. Philip Zimbardo acted as an expert witness at his trial, and claimed that, as with the subjects of the Stanford Prison

Experiment, Frederick was an ordinary man and a model citizen. He 'brought *no* pathology into that situation. There is absolutely nothing in his record that I was able to uncover that would predict that Chip Frederick would engage in any form of abusive, sadistic behaviour. On the contrary, had he not been forced to work and live in such an abnormal situation, he might have been the military's All American poster soldier on its recruitment ads.'[20]

That shifts the blame on to circumstances and ignores the place of human responsibility and free will, but it does serve to show that decent people may not always be as strong as they like to think. Sadly, of course, Abu Ghraib is not the only example of such regressive and abusive behaviour that can be evidenced in almost every period of human history.

The force of personality

Myra Hindley was one of the most notorious serial killers in modern times. With her partner Ian Brady she was convicted of the 'Moors murders' in which five children and young people were abducted, raped and killed in cold blood before being buried in remote areas on the Yorkshire moors between 1963 and 1965.

One day soon after the first murder, Myra Hindley opened her door to a good-looking policeman, Norman Sutton. At the time she wasn't a suspect, and there is no record of her reaction when she saw him. He had called about her van, offering to buy it. Something drew her to him and she began a short affair with him, which led Hindley to consider joining the police force. They obviously got on well, but she didn't – or couldn't – break with Ian Brady. She had fallen under his spell.

Years later, she wrote, 'If we'd [Sutton and she] met before Ian and I did, I knew that the love that had grown between us would have blossomed. I would have had no hesitation in marrying and having children with him.'[21] Myra Hindley had always been headstrong and tough, someone who wasn't afraid to fight back physically against those who annoyed her. But she also had a softer side. She was for years – even during the period of the murders – a woman who babysat for neighbours and got on superbly well with children who never came to any harm.

But she had already made a fatal choice. Her relationship with Brady had both exposed and nurtured the dark side of her nature. Brady introduced her to nihilistic literature, and talked with her about planning the perfect crime – initially robbery, but later murder. He was clearly a hypnotic and controlling character; but she was also a willing listener and learner.

He awoke something in her that excited and drove her, and seemed to drain the 'normality' that she had previously exhibited. By the time of her arrest and trial, she came across as cold and unfeeling. Some people claimed that she recovered her humanity while in prison (others dispute it), but by then it was far too late. The damage was done, and she died a prisoner.

'Not me, Lord!'

It would be easy to dismiss the people in these examples as 'easily led' or 'weak-willed'. We like to think that we'd be strong, perceptive. So before we leave this, it's important to note that one of the key figures in the New Testament and leaders of the early church, Peter, twice caved in to pressure. The first was his well-known capitulation in front of a barmaid while Jesus was on trial down the road. He denied knowing the Jesus he had once called 'The Christ, the Son of the living God'.[22]

The second was well after the anointing of the Holy Spirit on the Day of Pentecost. Peter was an established missionary through whom the first non-Jews (Gentiles) became Christians. Suddenly he refused to associate with Gentiles, 'because he was afraid of those who belonged to the circumcision group' – a pressure group of influential Jewish-Christians who had not yet understood that in the Christian church 'there is neither Jew nor Greek, slave nor free, male nor female, for you are all one in Christ Jesus'.[23]

He received a stiff rebuke from fellow apostle Paul, and it was perhaps with this in mind that Paul wrote not long afterwards, 'If you think you are standing firm, be careful that you don't fall!'[24] We can probably identify with that. Pressure is hard to resist. We go with the crowd, and might end up where we never intended.

Our third category of 'normal' person is harder to understand.

Type 3: The power-crazy person

In this section you will discover that, like Myra Hindley, two infamous tyrants of modern times had another, human side to their characters. It is important to point out that highlighting these is not to minimise the evils they perpetuated. Rather it illustrates how some people can be grossly inconsistent. Knowing this may help us to think about how we react to inconsistent people closer to home. But at this stage we are just observing puzzling facts that in many ways we would prefer to ignore. Reactions will be explored later.

One day in 1975, Heidi Holland, a South African journalist, received at short notice a surprise dinner guest. He was Robert Mugabe, recently released from detention and on his way to Mozambique. The visit was short because Mugabe was late. The taxi to take him to the station after the meal never arrived. So Ms Holland left her toddler sleeping alone in the apartment and drove Mugabe to catch his train. The next day he phoned her to thank her for the meal and lift, and to ask if the child was safe.

More than 30 years later she wrote what she called a 'psychobiography' of Mugabe, who by then was President of Zimbabwe and one of the world's most notorious tyrants.[25] His long and brutal reign reduced a once prosperous country to poverty. Heidi Holland interviewed scores of people who had known Mugabe at various times, and consulted psychologists in the process. She also had a rare opportunity to interview Mugabe himself shortly before publication. She wanted to understand why the quiet boy who had been an exemplary and studious Roman Catholic had changed so much.

In his younger days he had modelled himself on the courtly manners of upper-class English people and was considered by many to be a perfect gentleman. His first wife's family recalled him as 'wonderfully polite and gentle', and when he was in prison he replied thoughtfully to letters from a child (his niece by marriage) as any good and caring uncle might.

Mixed in with the later accounts of violence and oppression, Heidi Holland found further evidence of this human side. 'A nun in St Anne's Hospital, where Bona Mugabe [Robert's mother] stayed when she was ill and where she eventually died, remembers him bringing flowers not only for his mother but for the nurses as well.' According to a priest, 'Mugabe in going to great lengths to help fellow detainees, had a good heart in the prison years. He risked his life to thank Sister Lamb for her support during the bush war [when he was on the run] ... Later, once ensconced at State

House, he gave lessons to illiterate members of his household staff to help them pass exams.'[26]

That was not all. Mac McGuiness was a high-ranking secret service officer under Ian Smith, the former leader of Rhodesia until Mugabe took over the renamed country after independence. 'Mugabe is the only politician among the many I have met who kept his word,' McGuiness told her. 'He undertook at independence to let bygones be bygones and he never lifted a finger against his former enemies, including Ian Smith, who was allowed to live in Zimbabwe as long as he pleased and to criticise Mugabe whenever he chose for the rest of his life. He was more generous to Smith than Smith was to him.'[27] But somewhere down the line, it all went sour. Mugabe became a paranoid ruler of a brutal regime, and many white landowners were subjected to land-grabs and violence.

It was a similar story with Adolf Hitler, whose hatred of the Jews led to the slaughter of some six million of them in the Second World War. Some people who knew him when he was young described him as a pleasant and gentle youth, although he tended to be a loner and had exhibited eccentricities and excitability as a student. In private he was often kindly to his young relatives and his staff. Rosa Mitterer, who worked for Hitler as a maid, said of him, 'He was a charming man, someone who was only ever nice to me, a great boss to work for. You can say what you like but he was a good man to us.'[28]

Among many who have tried to make sense of Hitler, Yehuda Bauer, founder and chairman of the Department of Holocaust Studies at the Hebrew University, Jerusalem, described him as 'evil' (as opposed to 'insane'), but '*not* inhuman – that's the problem we have with them [the Nazis] because they are like us and we are like them'.[29]

Before we react instantly, 'No we're not' (and before we remember the 'office Hitler' who makes our life a misery at work), we are simply noting that just as the moon is always facing the earth in one way and has another, hidden side, so it is for every human being – including the tyrants who wreak havoc. However, the side most of us see is the dark one; hidden from view is the softer, lighter side, the vestiges of humanity that are observed only by a few close relatives or associates. The uncomfortable truth is that most of us are walking contradictions. We all have those two sides.

Paul recognised this in an outburst of anguish at his own contradictory nature: 'I have the desire to do what is good, but I cannot carry it out. For I do not do the good I want to do, but the evil I do not want to do – this I keep on doing.'[30] Theologians call this the effect of 'the Fall'. Basically, we're not perfect and we are vulnerable. 'Sin' is a constant companion in this life, but it's only one aspect of our personality.

Social psychologist Philip Zimbardo suggests that 'each of us has the capacity to be a saint or a sinner, altruistic or selfish, gentle or cruel, dominant or submissive, perpetrator or victim, prisoner or guard. Maybe it is our social circumstances that determine which of our many mental templates, our potentials, we develop.'[31]

So be warned. Human nature isn't as black and white as we like to think. But before we leave this survey there is one final type of 'normal' people who are simply consummate actors – and recognising them is extremely difficult, until they have wreaked their damage.

Type 4: The duplicitous person

'Doctor Jack' couldn't believe what was happening. A criminal leader of the notorious Bandidos biker gangs in North America, he had trusted and mentored fellow gang member Alex Caine. But Jack had just been arrested, and Caine was testifying against him. Jack asked Caine why he had turned.

'"Jack, I didn't turn," I told him. "I was hired from the start to get you guys. I was never the guy you thought I was. That guy never existed."' Caine had been working undercover for the police, patiently over a long period, collecting evidence and wearing a wire to record incriminating conversations. Yet he had been perfectly assimilated into gang culture, and the natural suspicions of him when he was a newcomer had long been abandoned. He wasn't what he seemed. He was playing a part to perfection.

In Caine's case, we can be thankful that there are such people prepared to take huge personal risks to gather the kind of evidence that would enable a jury to convict a criminal 'beyond all reasonable doubt'. Their work does come at a cost. Caine almost went native but got out in time, yet he still retains the regalia of his membership and came to regard the Bandidos as his family.[32]

What is generally impossible to approve is the deliberate double life of people who betray our country's secrets. (Others, of course, see them as heroes.) Anthony Blunt was one of the 'Cambridge Five' group of British spies who gave information to Russia in the 1940s. Like the others (Kim Philby, Guy Burgess, Donald Maclean and John Cairncross), Blunt was recruited to the communist cause while a student at Cambridge.

He later became an outstanding art historian. During the Second World War he joined MI5 (the counter-espionage and counter-terrorism agency). There he was responsible for surveillance of foreign embassies in London, and apart from the valuable information that provided, he was able to pick up more from colleagues and duly pass what he knew to his Russian controller.

After the war he returned to the art world. He became Keeper of the Royal Pictures in 1945 and was knighted in 1956. By the time he confessed to his treachery in 1964 he had published numerous books, including a minor classic on seventeenth-century French art. As Director of the Courtauld Institute he transformed it 'from a finishing school for wealthy young men and women into the powerhouse of British art history'. He was Professor of the History of Art at London University, and worked with the Queen to open a gallery of pictures from the royal collection.[33]

The truth finally became public in 1979 (he was not prosecuted in 1964 and continued with much of his art work). People who knew him were astounded. Lord Victor Rothschild, a brilliant zoologist and heir to the banking family, was a close friend of Blunt and had recruited him into the security service. He had once described Blunt as 'a saint'. 'I found it almost impossible to believe' that Blunt had been a Soviet agent, he said.[34]

Senior MI5 officer Dick White (who was head of MI5 from 1953 to 1956), said, 'He was a very nice and civilised man and I enjoyed talking to him. You cannot imagine how it feels to be betrayed by someone you have worked side by side with unless you have been through it yourself.'[35]

A secretary at MI5 put it more graphically: 'He was a charmer! Poor Anthony! We were all a bit in love with Anthony.' When his treachery was revealed she said, 'It was exactly like being in an earthquake – or on a quicksand, I couldn't believe it … I mean the whole world shook. It really shook for me.'

Another recalled, 'You couldn't fault him in any way. And I was absolutely astounded [when news of his treachery] broke. Incredible!'[36]

When Blunt died in 1983, John Pope-Hennessy, Professor of Fine Arts at New York University, paid him a moving tribute. 'He will be remembered, I hope, not only for his scholarship but for the scholarly work he sponsored, even financed and in which he was happy to let others take the credit. His achievements were wide … I hope it is not as Shakespeare once said … "the evil that men do lives after them, the good is oft interred with their bones."'[37]

Was Judas also an agent in place, working undercover for the religious or political authorities at the time of his recruitment by Jesus? It's safe to answer no. There is no evidence that Judas had been reporting to them until the night he decided to change sides. When Judas became an apostle, Jesus was virtually unknown, one of several unorthodox teachers offering spiritual enlightenment. There was no reason for the authorities to infiltrate this small group of Galileans until much later when the crowds began to adulate Jesus.

Other than for national security purposes, deliberately living a double life cannot be regarded as an acceptable lifestyle. Paul tells the inconsistent members of the church in Corinth, 'We have renounced secret and shameful ways; we do not use deception, nor do we distort the word of God.'[38]

The model is Nathanael, recognised by Jesus as transparent: 'Here is a true Israelite, in whom there is no deceit.'[39] Unfortunately, hypocrisy – the term is derived from the Greek word for an actor – comes very easily to most of us.

We put on a face or assume a pose in order to please, influence, impress or control whomever we encounter.

'What you see is what you get', sadly, is more likely to be true of a computer program than a human being. 'Do not lie to each other,' Paul cautions, 'since you have taken off your old self with its practices and have put on the new self, which is being renewed in knowledge in the image of its Creator.' And the ancient psalmist prayed, 'give me an undivided heart'.[40]

Unfortunately, such transparency is not always practised even within churches. Upright and welcoming church-wardens on Sunday can transform into uptight bullies in their workplace on Monday. Kindly choirmasters or scout leaders with infinite patience can befriend grateful families and win the confidence of their children before sexually abusing their young charges.

It's enough to destroy our faith in humanity. But it need – should – not. It's time to react, thoughtfully.

A fresh perspective

The examples we've looked at are mostly extreme and distant from us. We react to them with shock, perhaps, or disgust. We rightly expect the full force of the law to be brought against tyrannical and traitorous people (and nothing which follows denies that). Mostly we tend not to dwell on them.

It's not so easy to distance ourselves from bad situations which touch us more personally. A friend leaves his wife and young children and sets up home with a new partner, leaving a trail of emotional suffering and physical upheaval. A relative is jailed for theft, fraud or murder, throwing the wider family into conflict and confusion. A long-standing work colleague suddenly turns nasty and as a result of their politicking you are marginalised in the company. A neighbour blocks your access because of a dispute over a tree that overhangs their property. Serious or petty, we all know situations where formerly sweet people turn sour.

So how do we regard such people? The way we think will directly affect the way we react. The natural and understandable reaction is anger (once we've got over the sheer disbelief that such a thing has happened). Fuelled by anger, we may lash out in some way. We may ostracise the perpetrator, seek revenge, hit back. We may write them off as a waste of space, a monster, an evil swine, and tell as many people as we can just what they are really like.

Reactions like that may help us to feel better, but generally they only add to the sum total of bad feeling, mistrust and antisocial behaviour that already exists in the world. Real life starts to imitate the make-believe world of TV soaps which centre on arguments and disputes.

This does little to bring healing and peace, to ourselves or others. Such reactions, writes one Bible commentator, 'depress those against whom they are directed, and weaken rather than strengthen their moral fibre. They also increase the self-righteousness of those who [so react], and invite others to retaliate by indulging in equal measure in the same type of nagging fault-finding.'[41]

There is a better way. It requires us to think counter-intuitively. Not with scathing condemnation but with searching curiosity. It is the way of Jesus, often applauded but not so often applied. In Jesus' famous Sermon on the Mount he claims that happiness comes from thinking and doing virtually the opposite of what many of us take for granted.

German theologian Helmut Thielicke commented that 'anybody who enters into fellowship with Jesus must undergo a transvaluation of values'.[42] In other words, we have to be prepared for what St Paul calls 'the renewing of your mind',[43] which we'll consider in more detail later. It means looking at things from a wider point of view, and recognising, humbly, that we can never really get inside the head of another person to know all the complex influences that have led to their action.

So, says Jesus, 'Do not judge.'[44] 'Judge' here means to be 'censorious'. It refers to carping criticism, scornful rejection, hate-filled reaction, harsh condemnation. It is not an instruction to lay aside the distinction between right and wrong, nor to overlook palpable crimes and serious moral lapses. That would lead to anarchy, not order, and God is 'not a God of disorder but of peace'.[45] Rather, it is a call for a new way of regarding human failure.

'The censorious critic is a fault-finder who is negative and destructive towards other people and enjoys actively seeking out their failings,' says commentator John Stott. 'He puts the worst possible construction on their motives, pours cold water on their schemes, and is ungenerous towards their mistakes.'[46]

And shining the spotlight right into the censorious mind, spiritual writer Martin Laird suggests that it reveals 'a mass of anger, fear, envy, pride and shame'.[47] Perhaps that is why Jesus continued his little talk about censoriousness by using the famous metaphor of trying to remove a speck from someone's eye while ignoring the plank in one's own. 'For in the same way as you judge others, you will be judged, and with the measure you use, it will be measured to you.'[48]

Jesus' concern is for our mental, emotional and spiritual health; anger and its associated thoughts and emotions are decidedly unhealthy. They damage us and do nothing to alleviate the damage done by others.

The term 'measure' reflects the view of first-century Jewish rabbis that God had two 'measures' by which he judged the world: mercy and justice. It is a dispassionate assessment of a person's actions on the basis of a full and complete knowledge of their circumstances, limitations, motivations and understandings, on their whole personhood – and only God has that kind of comprehensive viewpoint.

Towards compassion

In many cases it is impossible for us to understand, let alone undo or unravel, the complex circumstances that may have contributed to any particular situation. But trying to understand them may help us to handle such issues (and our own faults) more creatively. We can take three initial steps.

Put yourself in their shoes

Madeleine Albright, US Secretary of State during the Clinton administration, has written about conflict resolution: 'In any conflict reconciliation becomes possible when the antagonists cease dehumanising each another and begin instead to see a bit of themselves in their enemy. That is why it is a standard negotiating technique to ask each side to stand in the shoes of the other … Effective foreign policy requires that we comprehend why others act as they do'.[49]

Putting ourselves into others' shoes by asking what may have led them to think and act the way they have done is the foundation for any progress towards dealing with bad things. If it is 'standard negotiating technique' at the international level, it ought to be a natural reflex at the personal level.

Remember their shared humanity

Among the alleged last words of Che Guevara, the Argentinian Marxist revolutionary who rose to prominence in Cuba and led militant movements elsewhere in Latin America, were to his executioner: 'Remember, you are killing a man.'[50]

Whatever someone has done, however much suffering they may have caused, they are still a human being – as we have seen earlier in some of the more extreme cases of tyrannical behaviour. There is something different about people, compared to other living creatures. We explain it theologically by referring to the concept of people being made 'in the image of God'[51] – rational, feeling, creative and spiritual beings with a unique dignity. Their humanity is a reason to be cautious in our assessment of them, however inhumane we consider their actions to have been.

Remember your own failings

We saw above how Jesus cautioned against censoriousness because we each have our own failings. The apostle James cuts through the usual excuse that we're not as bad as others by pointing out that the person who 'keeps the whole law and yet stumbles at just one point is guilty of breaking all of it'.[52] Wrong is wrong, he means, and there is no sliding scale of seriousness, however much we rightly differentiate between wrongs within secular legal systems. In St Paul's blunt terms, 'the wages of sin is death'; any wrong diminishes us – may even destroy us – spiritually.[53]

Finding a better way

St Paul never minced his words when he confronted people whose Christian lives or teachings failed to match up to his exacting standards. 'Watch out for those dogs, those evildoers, those mutilators of the flesh,' he warned the Philippians. But he goes on, 'I have often told you before and now *tell you again even with tears*, many live as enemies of the cross of Christ.'[54]

He doesn't despise them; he despairs for them. His attitude is one of concern, not condemnation. He knows that no one is beyond redemption, that anyone can see the error of their ways and do something to repair the damage they have caused. 'The truth must be married to love,' writes one commentator on this passage. 'How easy it would be to import into our reading of these words the harshness which we would feel towards people whom we judged worthy of such names! But even as Paul denounces ... he weeps for their souls ... In Paul we see the perfect marriage of truth and love, and this also is part of his example bequeathed to us.'[55]

Love, or at least compassionate understanding, is more powerful than hate, because it has the power to transform lives, as Joanne Jaffe discovered in New York City. She was head of police in a crime-ridden area in 2003 where some 100 juveniles were responsible for most of the robberies. She stepped up surveillance, recruited 'cops who love kids', and tried to get to know the offenders' families.

Initial approaches failed, so she began thinking outside the box. She used public funds to buy Thanksgiving turkeys for all the offenders' families. Her team delivered them personally with the message, 'I know you sometimes hate the police. I understand all that. But I just want you to know ...

we really do care, and we really do want you to have a happy Thanksgiving.'

They were warmly received. Then her team started to play basketball with the kids, help them get jobs, drive them to doctors' appointments, and they even held a Christmas dinner for the families. And over the next five years, the number of robberies steadily dropped. She had treated actual and potential criminals as human beings, and they responded with greater respect and cooperation. Most of the offenders, in fact, were pretty normal people.[56]

There *are* alternative, creative ways of dealing with difficult people and situations. Even when you, or they, are a newcomer and considered to be an 'outsider'.

Notes

[1] Alexander Solzhenitsyn, *The Gulag Archipelago*, Collins/Fontana, 1974, p.168.

[2] John 12:6.

[3] John 6:71, my italics.

[4] Luke 6:16, my italics.

[5] Luke 9:1-2, 10; compare 10:17.

[6] C. H. Spurgeon, *Treasury of the New Testament, vol. 2*, Marshall, Morgan and Scott (nd), p.499; in the context of John 13:23-26.

[7] John 6:64.

[8] Matthew 16:13-17.

[9] Matthew 16:23.

[10] 1 Timothy 1:19.

[11] Hebrews 4:11; 10:26-27.

[12] 2 Samuel 11–12.

[13] Matthew 21:9; 22:42

[14] Luke 10:25-37.

[15] Described by Cordelia Fine, *A Mind of its Own*, Icon Books, 2007, pp.68ff.

[16] Reported in *The Shropshire Star*, 24th March 2015.

[17] 1 Corinthians 15:33.

[18] The story of 101 Battalion is told in Christopher Browning, *Ordinary Men*, Penguin Books, 2001. The quotation is from p.161.

[19] The story of the experiment is told in Philip Zimbardo, *The Lucifer Effect*, Rider, 2009.

[20] Ibid., p.344

[21] Quoted from Emlyn Williams, *Beyond Belief* (Pan Books, 1968, p.27) by Carol Ann Lee, *One of Your Own*, Mainstream, 2011, p.128.

[22] John 18:15-18, 25-27.

[23] Galatians 2:12; 3:28.

[24] 1 Corinthians 10:12.

[25] Heidi Holland, *Dinner with Mugabe*, Penguin Books, 2008.

[26] Ibid., pp. 153f.

[27] Ibid., p.36.

[28] Quoted by A. N. Wilson, *Hitler: A Short Biography*, Harper Press, 2012, p.70.

[29] Quoted by Ron Rosenbaum, *Explaining Hitler*, Macmillan, 1998, pp.280, 282.

[30] Romans 7:18-19.

[31] Philip Zimbardo, *op. cit.*, p.297.

[32] Alex Caine, *Befriend and Betray*, Mainstream Publishing, 2009.

[33] Details about the life and work of Anthony Blunt can be found in Barrie Penrose and Simon Freeman, *Conspiracy of Silence*, Grafton Books, 1986. Further details are in Christopher Andrew, *The Defence of the Realm*, Allen Lane, 2009.

[34] Penrose and Freeman, *op. cit.*, p.141.

[35] Ibid., p.251.

[36] Both quotes in this paragraph are recorded by Christopher Andrew, *op. cit.*, p.270.

[37] Penrose and Freeman, *op. cit.* p.543.

[38] 2 Corinthians 4:2.

[39] John 1:47.

[40] Colossians 3:9-10; Psalm 86:11.

[41] R. V. G. Tasker, *The Gospel According to St Matthew*, The Tyndale Press, 1961, p.79, altered.

[42] Quoted by John Stott in *Christian Counter-culture*, InterVarsity Press, 1978, p.55.

[43] Romans 12:1-2.

[44] Matthew 7:1.

[45] 1 Corinthians 14:33.

[46] Stott, ibid., p.176.

[47] Martin Laird, *Into the Silent Land*, Darton, Longman & Todd, 2006, p.126.

[48] Matthew 7:2.

[49] Madeleine Albright, *The Mighty and the Almighty*, Macmillan, 2006, pp.72f.

[50] Quoted by Tim Weiner, *Legacy of Ashes*, Allen Lane, 2007, p.283.

[51] Genesis 1:27.

[52] James 2:10.

[53] Romans 6:23; the passage continues 'but the gift of God is eternal life'. Paul is writing about hope and renewal in the face of human sinfulness.

[54] Philippians 3:2, 18; my italics.

[55] Alec Motyer, *The Richness of Christ*, InterVarsity Fellowship, 1966, p.145.

[56] The story is given in greater detail in Malcolm Gladwell's *David and Goliath*, Allen Lane, 2013, pp.209-217.

Chapter 2
Treading the lonely road

People who feel alone, rejected, outcast, or just 'different' are sometimes prone to thoughts and actions which reinforce rather than remedy their aloneness. Here we examine various types of 'outsider', and ask how we can help ourselves or others to feel valued and integrated.

To betray you must first belong. I never belonged.
(Kim Philby)[1]

The human mind is wonderfully inventive. Our unique ability to reflect and imagine is the source of creativity in the arts, sciences and community development. But it can also play tricks on us. Feeling for some reason that we are 'different', struggling to forge meaningful relationships, smarting from rejection or failure, experiencing disruptive family life or other adverse circumstances: what life throws at us can send our minds spiralling into freefall. Our inner agonies can drive our creative abilities not into positive directions but down destructive avenues.

Chris Harper-Mercer was shot dead by police after the 26-year-old had gunned down nine people in Umpqua Community College in Roseberg, Oregon. It was one of the more recent incidents of mass killing in the United States.

What made this especially noteworthy was the apparent background and writings of the perpetrator.

According to reports, Harper-Mercer, who had been born in the US but had British parents and passport, was allegedly an introverted and skittish person who had been rejected by the US army after a month of basic training. On a blog site to which he apparently contributed (the entry was connected to his email address), he had reflected on another killer, Vester Flanagan, who not long before had killed two TV crew in cold blood while they were doing their job.

He noted how an unknown person could suddenly become famous through such an atrocity. 'His face is splashed across every screen, his name across the lips of every person on the planet, all in the course of one day,' he wrote. 'People like him have nothing left to live for, and the only thing left to do is lash out at a society that has abandoned them.'[2] Harper-Mercer also seems to have thought of himself as a loner, an outsider.

There are many such stories of people who have similarly lashed out destructively and indiscriminately because of their frustration with, and perceived alienation from, others. In a busy, competitive and impersonal society, the desire to make a mark on the world, to be considered 'in' with a particular group, is strong. So too is the temptation to turn in on ourselves and react negatively when we don't make what others consider to be the grade. It need not be so – but sadly, it may have been so for Judas Iscariot.

The disciple outside

Judas was almost certainly 'different' to Jesus and the other 11 disciples. His surname suggests that he was a southerner, probably from the Judean settlement of Kerioth some 19 miles south-west of Jerusalem. (An alternative suggestion is Kir-Hareseth east of the Dead Sea and equally in the deep south of Judea.) In biblical times, surnames usually denoted either a person's father ('son of') or their place of origin. The latter is most likely in this case because John's gospel also applies Iscariot to Judas' father.[3]

That is certainly the view of most scholars, although there have been other suggestions about his name. Some have thought it might be a reference to the *Sicarii*, a loosely linked band of assassins bent on killing the Roman invaders with their hidden curved daggers.[4] But that stretches the language too far, and is unlikely to have been used as a nickname in the apostolic group. It would have glorified violence, which Jesus was opposed to, and would have attracted unwelcome attention from the Romans.

Most if not all the other disciples, and Jesus himself, were northerners from around Galilee. And, just as with the north–south divides of the UK and the USA, there would have been clear differences between them. Judas would have had a different accent – the others would have considered that he talked 'posh' – and some of their colloquialisms would have sounded foreign to his ears.

Along with the regional *patois* there was a regional culture. The people of Galilee were more racially mixed than those of Judea, with Jews and Gentiles living and working in close proximity without discrimination between them. They tended to be more open to newcomers, and to new ideas. People in Judea tended to be more conservative, more wary of newcomers, less open to new ideas.

At least six of the other disciples were probably acquainted with one another before they met Jesus. There were two pairs of brothers (Andrew and Peter, James and John) who also knew each other from their fishing work. Philip came from

46

the same town so was probably acquainted with them, and he in turn introduced his friend Nathanael (believed to be Bartholomew in some of the lists of disciples) to Jesus. Matthew was called by Jesus from his customs post which was also in Galilee, so he probably also shared the same local background.

We don't know the provenance of the other four (Thomas, James son of Alphaeus, Thaddaeus also known as Judas the son of James, and Simon the Zealot), but even if one or other of these was from down south, Judas Iscariot would still have felt in a small minority. Peter, it seems, was the spokesman and leader (under Jesus) of the group, an outspoken and blunt man whose Galilean personality would have coloured the character of the whole group. It would not have been easy for a stranger and outsider to fit in.[5]

Of course, Judas must have been attracted to Jesus or he would never have become a close follower. And Jesus must have seen some potential in Judas (tradition has it that Judas was well educated and close to the religious establishment, but there is no way of proving this). Perhaps Judas saw in Jesus a teacher with real potential to reform the rather staid religious establishment from which he came. Or, perhaps, as a refreshing voice in the wilderness who would shake up the political stalemate.

But whatever his reasons, it's easy to imagine that in a group of 13 men, living and working in close proximity, there would be inevitable banter (and at stressful times, irritation) highlighting differences in personality and lifestyle. Judas might well have been ribbed for his accent. He might have reacted with genuine good humour, or tolerated the jokes and slowly built up a resentful antagonism to the group.

Perhaps too he struggled to cast aside the constraints inherited from his background and embrace the more liberal views of the Galileans. He may once have hoped to initiate them into the more refined ways of the southerners, and became frustrated and angry when they never quite saw things his way. Perhaps such thoughts simmered until they boiled over, and he took the impetuous and irrevocable steps to hand Jesus over to the authorities.

We can only speculate. But we do know that similar scenarios are common.

The angst of the incomer

Human beings are naturally social creatures. We were made – hard-wired – that way. In the biblical account of creation God says of Adam, 'It is not good for the man to be alone. I will make a helper suitable for him.'[6] Although there can be times when isolation from the demands of society and the intrigues of people might seem highly attractive, enforced periods of aloneness are generally debilitating. As W. H. Auden wrote at the end of his poem about a mail train, 'For who can bear to feel himself forgotten?'[7]

Who indeed? The novelist Daniel Defoe identified the long-term agony of isolation in his morality tale *Robinson Crusoe*. The sole survivor of a shipwreck on a desert island was able to become self-sufficient, but he began to plan a means of escape because, 'What I so earnestly longed for,' he said, was 'somebody to speak to, and to learn some knowledge from of the place where I was.'[8]

It is never easy to move into a new place: new school, starting college, fresh job, joining a club, moving house. Sometimes you may be welcomed, supported, shown the ropes, befriended. At other times it's like going into a crowded room where everyone else is gathered into clusters, talking animatedly. Which cluster do you join? How do you break into the conversation?

Some people will simply dive in, compensating in various ways for their awkwardness in their attempts to be accepted by others. Talking loudly, perhaps, telling risqué jokes, spinning stories (not necessarily completely accurate) about their achievements or credentials. In so doing they risk being seen as a bore, but they may also be drawn in to groups of like-minded people.

Others, less anxious to be accepted at once, may let their skills (in sport, study or work) do the talking until people are drawn to them, valuing their contribution and wanting to be associated with them. Some will hang around at the edges, waiting (sometimes vainly) for someone to spot them and take the initiative. When that doesn't happen, they may retreat into their shell, with a simmering sense of being unwanted, unloved inside them.

Such a feeling is a danger signal. It can prompt two unhealthy reactions. One is that we retreat further into ourselves and become more isolated, brooding on our unhappy state. We can sink into depression and find ourselves unable to summon up the energy and initiative to interact effectively with others – a vicious circle that is hard to break. The other is that we try to 'put one over' on people, or get revenge in some way.

Klaus Fuchs, later dubbed 'the atom spy', seems to have been such a person. He was the son of a Lutheran pastor in Germany. Fuchs came to Britain as a refugee from the Nazis in the 1930s. 'He learned now to do without ties to other people, and withdraw into himself,' suggests his biographer. Yet he kept letters he had received for years, 'as if, with his limited human contact, he wanted those tangible signs of the contact he did have.'[9] He was a talented scientist and was recruited into the team developing Britain's atomic bomb. He had been a socialist in Germany, had joined the communist party when the socialist movement broke down, then disowned his country when the Nazis came to power. Despite receiving UK citizenship he never considered himself British either. In this stateless existence, of belonging nowhere, he felt he owed loyalty to no one. So he leaked many of Britain's atomic secrets to the Russians.

Of course, Fuchs' rootlessness was not the only factor. No one acts as they do for single, isolated reasons – which is why we cannot nail Judas' betrayal down to one causal factor. Fuchs was a complex person; his mother had committed suicide when he was 19, as had her mother and one of his sisters; another sister ended up in a mental hospital. In confessing to his double dealings later, he claimed he had divided his mind comfortably into 'two separate compartments', which he called 'controlled schizophrenia'.[10]

But his case – and others like it – illustrates the point that an incomer struggling to belong can ultimately act in a destructive way, causing harm to others as well as to themselves. However, some incomers do succeed in becoming integrated. Ayaan Hirsi Ali is one.

The daughter of a Somalian political activist, Ayaan moved as a child first to Saudi Arabia, then to Ethiopia and finally to Kenya, where her father left the family. Aged 22, she was ordered by her Muslim family to marry a cousin she had never met in Toronto, Canada.

On the way, she fled to the Netherlands, where she 'discovered the kindness of strangers'. She learned the language, worked her way through university and became a Dutch politician. Then she had to leave when her immigration status was questioned, and she fled again, this time to the

USA. Once more, now aged 38, she felt that she was a nomad, a wanderer, an outsider.

'I had escaped from my family and gone to Europe because I hadn't wanted to be trapped in marriage to a virtual stranger I didn't like,' she reflected. 'Now, in America, I felt rootless, lost. To be a nomad, always wandering, had always sounded romantic. In practice, to be homeless and living out of a suitcase was a little foretaste of hell.'[11]

But Ayaan was, and is, a determined woman and now has dual Dutch–US citizenship, is married to the British historian Niall Ferguson, and is a passionate advocate of human rights. She is openly critical of the attitude of Islam to women, and has become an atheist. But that hasn't stopped her from affirming one feature of Christianity as a potential contribution to a harmonious world. 'The Christianity of love and tolerance remains one of the West's most powerful antidotes to the Islam of hate and intolerance,' she writes.[12]

Love and tolerance and the kindness of strangers is a virtue advocated in both the Old and New Testaments. How we might effect that welcome we shall consider later in the chapter. But if we are on the receiving end of coldness and indifference, what can we do about it? There is no universal remedy because everyone is different. But there are basic principles to consider when we find ourself an 'incomer':

- Be patient. Don't rush in to try to win friends and influence people; most of us are suspicious of pushy people.

- Be yourself. Don't put on an act; people soon spot a phoney.

- Accept invitations. A few may be inappropriate and some may take you out of your comfort zone, but they show that people are making an effort (for which show your appreciation), and by accepting some your awareness of your new situation will broaden.

- Be proactive. Find out from local media, libraries, notice boards about the facilities and opportunities that exist, and try some out. Try a church; generally newcomers are welcomed but not pressurised.

- Talk to people. Taking an interest in them may encourage them to take an interest in you.

- Above all, don't judge if you feel you are 'not wanted'. It was with good reason that Jesus said, 'Do not judge, or you too will be judged.'[13] Being judgemental increases the antagonism we feel to others, feeds the desire to hit out against them, and increases their hostility towards us.

The problems become even more acute for the person who once was 'in', and is then rejected.

The agony of the outcast

Mary Shelley's classic horror story *Frankenstein* is a powerful morality tale about human beings playing God, and the agony of being an outcast or just 'different'.

Having discovered how to reanimate dead creatures, Dr Frankenstein sews together various salvaged body parts to create a man. The 'monster' is born. Strangely articulate, the unattractive and oversized creature horrifies all who see him. They flee from him and try to kill him. Frustrated, he murders several people, including Frankenstein's fiancée on their wedding day. During various conversations, the creature – who was never given a name – explained why he was violent.

52

'I am malicious because I am miserable. Am I not shunned and hated by all mankind? … If any being felt emotions of benevolence towards me, I should return them an hundred and an hundred fold; for that one creature's sake, I would make peace with the whole kind!'

He pleads with Frankenstein to make a female with whom he could share his life, promising that they would be harmless ever after. Frankenstein refuses, and the slaughter continues. Having finally dispatched his creator as well, the creature tells Frankenstein's friend, 'Once I falsely hoped to meet with beings who, pardoning my outward form, would love me for the excellent qualities which I was capable of unfolding. I was nourished with high thoughts of honour and devotion. But now crime has degraded me beneath the meanest animal … I am alone.'[14]

I am alone. A nameless outcast. How many people have felt that desolation, that anonymity, that perceived rejection – and as a result have burned with a deep desire for acceptance and recompense? Anyone, in fact, who has been cursed by a callous teacher or a critical parent. Or rejected by a doctrinaire church leader or a judgemental employer disapproving of gender, sexuality, marital status, religious beliefs or criminal record. Or ridiculed by derisive peers who laughed at their physical or mental clumsiness and ineptitude. Or scorned by a jilting lover, partner or spouse. Or sacked without warning, explanation or support from a job they loved. Or abandoned by someone close, especially by the premature death of someone they relied on.

And how many socially integrated people have despised the outcasts and added to their pain? In August 2015 the *Daily Express* website broke with all human sensitivities and published '39 of the world's worst mugshots' of people 'with facial disfigurements alongside spiteful commentary'.

Despite long campaigns by disabled people for recognition and acceptance as fully human beings, people with physical or mental impairments, birth defects or disfigurements from accidents were depicted as a freak show to be laughed at. The item was quickly taken down and the company apologised, but that such an incident could happen at all suggests that the mentality that rejects people who are different remains close to the surface.[15]

The archetypal biblical outcast is Cain, the son of Adam and Eve and the brother of Abel. As the story goes, both brothers brought religious offerings to God. Abel, a herder and shepherd, brought a precious animal, costing him rather more in terms of personal sacrifice (animals were counted as units of wealth) than Cain's gleanings of fruit and grain from his crops. Abel's offering was an act and sign of commitment; Cain's was a token, formal gesture rather than an indicator of genuine gratitude and love towards God.

Cain was angry with God, who he felt was unreasonable, and perhaps he was also angry with life, which seemed to be offering him a raw deal. He was envious, too, of his younger brother's greater success and status. So he did what so many do: he took out his anger and frustration on someone else – his brother. He murdered him. And when he was asked about it by God, he merely shrugged it off with the famous rhetorical question: 'Am I my brother's keeper?' Who cares? He's not my concern.

The implied but silent response of the narrative is yes, Cain, you are his keeper; he is your concern, even if you currently hate the sight of him.

God punished Cain by banning him from a settled arable farming life and condemning him to become a nomad, a wanderer on the face of the earth. Cain suddenly realised the enormity of the consequences of his action. He knew that he would now be a target of both Abel's vengeful family and anyone else whose territory he trespassed on: 'They'll kill me!'

And then something quite extraordinary occurred. 'No,' said God, 'I won't let them.' He put a mark on Cain – a way of saying that God would protect Cain's life even though he would not – could not – undo the consequences of his action.[16]

This is not God going soft on crime, even though Cain has not explicitly apologised or expressed guilt – his concern is still for his own skin. This is God putting a brake on human wickedness, slowing the otherwise inevitable spiral from vengeance and self-interest into total chaos and anarchy. This is God saying that you have earned my disapproval and you will have to live with the consequences of your actions, but nonetheless you have a right to life, and I will not abandon you completely. God does not do what most of us would do – write Cain off. God never writes anyone off. No matter what they have done.

As one Bible commentator puts it, 'Even in this outer darkness, God's grace and mercy do not forsake his children. This is not the grace which chooses some and rejects others. It is the grace that will not let sin and evil completely have their way.'[17] Think about that. It's staggering. God pushes Cain to the margins yet still shows patience, concern, love even. To the outcast it is a message of hope: you are not totally abandoned.

And to everyone else it is a powerful challenge to the way we view outsiders. They too are human beings; our brothers, sisters, neighbours whom we are charged to love in the same way as we love ourselves. They have a God-given right to a life, and no one has the right to deprive them of it directly, or indirectly by ignoring their needs. We're called to be kind to strangers, and also to the people we label as 'strange'.

In Christian thought, God not only cares about the outcast, but he also becomes one himself. Jesus was born in a borrowed shelter. As a toddler he became a refugee fleeing a tyrannical leader. His adult experience was predicted centuries before by a poetic prophet and is regularly rehearsed by choral societies singing Handel's *Messiah*. 'He had no beauty or majesty to attract us to him, nothing in his appearance that we should desire him. He was despised and rejected by mankind, a man of suffering, and familiar with pain. Like one from whom people hide their faces he was despised, and we held him in low esteem.'[18]

That was agonisingly fulfilled as Jesus was sentenced to death by an indifferent judge in front of a howling mob. Hanging on the cross, he cried out in dire physical and emotional pain, 'My God, my God, why have you forsaken me?'[19]

God cannot be indifferent to the outcast. He is the lover of the unloved. There is always hope. To anyone feeling rejected and not knowing how to help themselves in practical terms, this may seem cold comfort. And this is why the responsibility is thrown on to the settled community to alleviate their distress. As James says bluntly in the New Testament, it's no good saying 'Go in peace; keep warm and well fed' yet doing nothing about their immediate needs, even if it is only through supporting local charities.[20]

Meanwhile, what can the outcast actually do? One thing is not to fall into the blame trap (even if, in fact, others have neglected their responsibilities). Blaming others only pushes us deeper into bitter resentment. It increases our anger, which at any moment could bubble over and affect not just the person or people who hurt us but a much wider circle too. Blame also magnifies our sense of helplessness; the more we blame others the less we are able to address our plight positively.

The people who have directly or indirectly contributed to our angst will have to answer to God and their own consciences for their thoughtless or callous actions. In some cases they will be unaware of the effect they have had on us; they were just blind to our needs or feelings, preoccupied with themselves. That's their problem, but only they can address it. The same applies, of course, to the angst we have caused others.

Rejection paralyses, and it's not surprising that outcasts sometimes deaden their despair with alcohol, drugs or socially destructive behaviour. But conversely, acceptance energises. It is easy to sound glib, and it's important not to tell anyone to 'snap out of it' or 'do something for yourself'. But it does help, emotionally and spiritually, to learn how to accept the present situation for what it is. Rejection was then but this is now: a new day, with potential new starts (and a supportive God in the wings).

The loner: fantasy forced into reality

A common way of dealing with our sense of aloneness is to daydream or to attempt to give ourselves a personality makeover. 'I spent the early part of my life trying to be someone else,' confessed business guru Charles Handy. 'At school I wanted to be a great athlete, at university an admired socialite, afterwards a businessman and, later, the head of a great institution. It did not take me long to discover that I was not destined to be successful in any of these guises, but that did not prevent me from trying, and being perpetually disappointed with myself.'[21]

He did later become a successful business professor, writer and broadcaster. Not everyone manages the degree of self-knowledge and musters the drive necessary to bridge the gulf between ambition and actualisation, between hopeless fantasy and humble fact. It is especially acute for teenagers forced to choose courses and hence potential careers before they are clear where their gifts and abilities lie, and for people who tend to be shy rather than outgoing.

Strategies to gain attention are often counterproductive. We don masks and end up like John le Carré's spy Ted Mundy musing as he walked the streets of Berlin. 'He no longer knows which parts of him are pretending. Perhaps all of him is. Perhaps he has never been anything but pretended man. A natural. A naturally pretended man.'[22]

Or we retreat into our own inner world, dreaming of what might have been, 'if only'. The online gaming industry (said now to be more profitable than the film industry) provides one way for people to immerse themselves in a fantasy world. There they find relief from the complex, disappointing and messy world of squabbles and rivalries, of complicated relationships and unfeeling authorities, of the everyday drudgery of making ends meet and loading the washing machine. They gain a sense of achievement and power as they succeed in quests, and a sense of belonging to an undemanding online community focused on the game.

Aldous Huxley, author of the famous *Brave New World*, once wrote, long before video games were thought of, that 'the world of mind is a comfortable Wombland, a place to which we flee from the bewildering queerness of the natural world'.[23]

Living in an imaginary parallel universe is distinctly unhealthy. It consumes our time, saps our energy and contributes nothing to the real needs of the human race. Worst of all, it infects us with the lie that we are someone else whom other people just won't recognise. Now and again, someone becomes so infected with that fantasy that they actively seek to turn their dream world into reality. That's when they really mess up.

Natascha Kampusch found that out at enormous and undeserved cost when a 'loner' snatched her off the street, aged ten, in Austria in March 1998. It was the first day she had walked to school on her own. Wolfgang Priklopil spotted her and bundled her into his van. He kept her in a cellar for eight years until she managed to escape, shortly after which he committed suicide without offering any reasons for his action.

However, a friend of the kidnapper, who was tried for aiding and abetting him, explained that the intention was to turn a young girl into a dream woman. 'Wolfgang had been unhappy since boyhood because no girl had ever fallen in love with him,' he told police. 'He was insecure about his looks.'[24]

That impression was confirmed by Natascha as she reflected on her ordeal. 'Today I believe that Wolfgang Priklopil, in committing a terrible crime, wanted to create nothing more than his own little perfect world with a person that could be there just for him … Basically, he didn't want anything more than anyone else: love, approval, warmth. He wanted somebody for whom he himself was the most important person in the world.'[25]

Sick, perhaps, but unable to achieve naturally what he wanted, he used force to fulfil his inner fantasies. In doing so, he abused Natascha, robbing her of both her childhood and her human dignity. To him, she was an object for his own fulfilment; what she felt and wanted from life seems never to have occurred to him.

Such self-preoccupation by a loner was evident in the horrific dictatorship exercised by German leader Adolf Hitler in the 1930s and 1940s. Despite the flashes of 'normality' we noted in the previous chapter, 'throughout his life he showed himself incapable of forming close personal friendships'. As a young aspiring artist living in a shelter for the homeless, 'he had no-one to talk to and withdrew more and more into himself'. A reading room circle gave him 'that degree of superficial contact which as a "loner" he needed, without compromising the reserve with which he surrounded himself, or involving him in any real human relationship.'[26]

He showed all the signs of what German-born psychologist Eric Fromm described as a classic narcissist – an introverted person dwelling in his own 'Wombland'. 'He is interested only in himself, *his* desires, *his* thoughts, *his* wishes; he talked endlessly about his ideas, his past, his plans; the world is interesting only as far as it is the object of his schemes and desires; other people matter only as far as they serve him or can be used; he always knows everything better than anyone else.'[27]

The same seems to be true for at least some more recent lone terrorists and gunmen. They harbour a grudge and, out of their narcissism, they vent their anger and frustration in deadly ways. Hitler, of course, has defied all attempts at explaining his phenomenal rise to power and the subsequent slaughter of some six million Jews. Offering any kind of explanation for a person's actions is in no way to excuse their excesses. The individual is personally responsible for what they do. Indeed, one writer has suggested that many of Hitler's biographers have let him off too lightly by focusing on the mad rather than the bad.[28]

However, narcissism is not far from each of us. While we would never go to such ruthless lengths as Priklopil or Hitler or frustrated or ideological murderers, most of us view ourselves as a bright sun around which most other people in our particular solar system are required to orbit. We deny it, of course, and can point to times when we have put someone else's needs before our own within our family or community. Yet often, and usually without thinking, we use other people for our own advancement or interest. We give no thought to their personality or needs. They are just there to serve us before we move on – like checkout assistants who save us the bother of scanning our purchases at the self-checkout, but might just as well be robots.

Beneath the family altruism and voluntary activity, my desires, thoughts, wishes, ideas and schemes remain priorities. It is inevitable, part of being human, a natural instinct to protect ourselves. If you don't believe it, just recall your recent eruptions of impatience or explosions of anger. Or the flashes of frustration and rumbles of resentment that tend to punctuate our busy, often stormy lives.

But (perhaps by way of temporary mitigation) our self-interest is also a product of a cultural change. From the middle of the twentieth century the autonomy of the individual has been promoted by politicians and advertisers almost to the exclusion of all else. One reason why the Old Testament of the Bible seems so far removed from contemporary life is that much of it reflects an opposite attitude. Community welfare, 'corporate solidarity' to give its technical name, is promoted above the interests of individuals. It talks more of personal responsibilities than of individual rights.

Yet it is not such a foreign concept. In social policy discussions it often parades under the name 'the common good', when a proposed course of action is believed to benefit many (although not necessarily all) people. One suggested form of intercession in the Anglican Church's *Common Worship* prays that God will 'give wisdom to all in authority; and direct this nation and every nation in the ways of justice and of peace; that we may honour one another and seek the common good'.

In the New Testament, self-interest is seen as a barrier to keep God at a safe distance. Even though humourless street preachers with doom-laden posters have made the concept of sin a laughing stock, in biblical terms sin is simply a shorthand for anything self-centred. By focusing excessively on my needs, my feelings, I become incapable of relating fully to God, and to the world and people around me.

The forgotten ones

In 2010, a 66-year-old woman in Cheshire died at home sitting in her chair. She had a dishcloth in her hand, and the gas fire was on. About 18 months later, the gas fire was still on and the dishcloth was still in her hand. Police broke down the door and discovered her body, which was so dried out that it was impossible to estimate accurately when she had died.[29]

Hers is not the only case of someone dying alone and lying undiscovered for some time, although she could hardly be classified as 'elderly', which is when the problem of living alone generally becomes more acute. Loneliness, and aloneness, is a growing problem in aging western populations. Better health care means we are all, on average, living longer than previous generations.

The charity Age UK estimates that five million older people regard the TV as their main companion, and that one million go for a week at a time without speaking to anyone. Studies suggest that loneliness can contribute to health problems, with the negative effect being the equivalent of smoking 15 cigarettes a day. Excessive consumption of alcohol – the world's favourite drug to deaden emotional pain – among older people is said to be on the rise.

Who has not stood in a supermarket queue behind a little old lady with two bottles of gin in her basket to go with her packet of fish fingers and bag of potatoes? TV personality Esther Rantzen was so rocked by her own sense of loneliness when her husband died – even though she has a supportive family – that she set up the Silverline helpline to assist people in a similar position.

It is also possible to be lonely in a crowd, especially in an impersonal city far from one's childhood home. Mental health issues among students, triggered by loneliness, homesickness and pressure to achieve, are on the increase. The problem is not made any easier by political, welfare and commercial systems that regard – and treat – individuals as undeserving digits in infallible databases. No wonder some overexert their individuality, and others fall into depression when they fail to find meaning to their lives.

Some 34 per cent of UK households are said to consist of one person. Widowhood and marital breakdown are obvious factors, but increased mobility has resulted in families and friends of all ages moving apart in search of jobs or housing. Opportunities to meet up are drastically reduced by distance and time constraints. The cliché 'out of sight, out of mind' soon kicks in, and previous contacts fade into the background, despite the availability of Skype and social media. Besides, electronic interaction is never as satisfying as a personal visit.

A common consequence of loneliness is boredom. There is a limit to the fulfilment a person can gain from daytime TV or online gaming. And boredom (which can be triggered by other factors as well as loneliness) can lead to socially destructive action.

Reflecting on both the Stanford Prison Experiment and the Abu Ghraib atrocities (outlined in chapter 1), Philip Zimbardo suggests that 'boredom operated in both prison settings, bred by long shift hours on those nights when everything was under control. Boredom was a potent motivator to take actions that might bring some excitement, some controlled sensation seeking. Both sets of guards decided on their own initiative "to make things happen" that they thought would be interesting or fun.'[30]

We see that in many towns and cities on a Saturday night as drunken youths, with nothing more creative to do, go on a rampage of intimidation and criminal damage. Gang culture (often linked to drugs and violence) is another attempt to create community by people who feel isolated or excluded.

So too is exhibitionism or self-promotion. The office clown seeking applause by performing stunts or mimicry; the pub philosopher holding court loudly, and putting down opposing views with witty scorn. A surprising number of showbiz performers suffer from personal insecurities which are at least partly compensated for by their stage and screen acts. British comedian Johnny Vegas once confessed that 'for all the hot air, the ranting and raving, Johnny's just a needy man who wants to be loved'.[31]

Apart from possible repercussions for the performer's own mental health, their angst is at least expressed in creative channels. But it can go wrong. Billie Piper was plucked from the streets of Swindon and launched from obscurity into stardom as 'the next Madonna' at the tender age of 15. She knew she wasn't that good and her singing voice was too weak, and over several years she fell into a spiral of self-destruction. Afraid to face her inner demons, alone in an adult world she wasn't ready for and inadequately supervised by those who sought to make money out of her, she became anorexic and headstrong.

'It's all about love,' she wrote. 'It's about someone giving you the biggest hug in the world and loving you. But of course you're being intolerable, pushing everyone to the limits, so you don't get the hug.'

She describes the vicious spiral graphically. Thinking that her problems were worse than anyone else's 'made me selfish. Selfishness isolates you, and isolation is lonely, and loneliness is destructive. Then you start doing stupid things that make it worse.'[32]

Selfishness isolates; isolation is lonely; loneliness is destructive. That almost deserves being written up next to 'love your neighbour as yourself' as a motto on everyone's kitchen board or fridge. It might have been a factor in Judas Iscariot's betrayal.

There are less-destructive, but not danger-free, ways in which we may seek to escape from today's endemic loneliness. Many get kudos from the number of Facebook or other social media 'friends' they amass, but such links are often superficial and ephemeral. Who will be there for them in person when they need practical help? Who will visit them in hospital, give them a place to stay or buy them food? Or who will ensure that if they do die suddenly, alone at home, they do not remain undiscovered, unmissed for 18 months? Most of us need to engage with others at deeper levels.

Internet chat rooms and dating sites have certainly helped some people find true love, but long-distance electronic relationships lack the natural checks and balances that exist when people befriend each other within a wider circle of acquaintances to whom both are known. Occasionally it can lead to disaster.

As I was writing this, a man was jailed for imprisoning a woman, the mother of young children, whom he had met online. They had been dating for some time without any problems, and the woman said that 'he seemed so lovely'. Then one day when she visited his home he became jealous and refused to let her leave. He took her phone and bank cards and treated her as a slave. After nine months she managed to escape through a window, breaking her ankle in the process.[33] More frequent are the cases of people being fleeced of their savings by sophisticated online contacts.

When we cannot escape loneliness, we can find positive strategies to turn it from a threat to an opportunity. The Archbishop of Canterbury's former Middle East envoy Terry Waite was held alone as a hostage in Lebanon for almost five years. Chained and in solitary confinement, he pleaded for books. When he was eventually given one, his isolation continued but his loneliness was partially addressed. 'Modern life is so fragmented, full of distractions,' he reflected. 'Here I can discover how to convert my loneliness into creative solitude. Part of the secret, I think, is to make a companion of the experience. Although much of my life has been spent alone, the real beauty of solitude is only now becoming apparent to me. If I ever leave captivity, I will take this precious gift with me.'[34]

Creative solitude

Most of us fear loneliness. We crave company. Of course, there are times when we want to get away from the bustle and clamour of crowds or family, but even then we tend to fill the silent vacuum with sound or activity. Increasingly at weekends or on holiday, people are checking work emails.

We fear being thought dispensable. We are afraid of missing something. We find it harder and harder to switch off.

In silent solitude we are cut off from distractions. Then we may become aware of dark, deep chasms of unknowingness that lurk in our minds and hearts. There are terrors there. Memories of past failures wait to leap out and flail us with guilt or regret. Knowledge of our present limitations bubbles like a lava lake, spitting hot anxieties at us. And future hopes and plans disappear into a dense, disorientating fog, making every decision hazardous. We really don't want to look down there.

Yet aloneness can be a friend, not an enemy. Every person needs that 'creative solitude'. Jesus regularly took time out alone to pray and ponder, even when the public were demanding his attention. When we don't stop, don't step back from the rush of everyday life, we can't see our big concerns in the context of an even greater picture. We risk getting those concerns, and our lives themselves, out of perspective. And then we risk taking wrong or potentially dangerous paths.

The spiritual writer Richard Foster suggests that 'distraction is one of the deepest problems we face today ... So in our day we must learn to be still. To wait. To hold our tongue. To observe. To ponder. To wonder. Silence cultivates the soil of our hearts so that life-giving words are allowed to germinate and take root. Then when the time comes for speaking, our words will flow like water from a silent spring.'[35]

'Be still, and know that I am God,' the psalmist ordered.[36] English translations typically take the sting out of the original Hebrew, which is much more pointed. 'Be still' is literally 'Stop! Shut up! Enough!' Even God can get fed up with our incessant chatter. We need to take time to listen to ourselves, to others and to God. From that may come creative ways in which we can reconnect with community. Suggestions as to how we might, in Terry Waite's words, 'make a companion of silence' are in the final chapter.

Welcome the stranger

Throughout this chapter has run a simple refrain: that it is the responsibility of the many to include the few, of the insider to embrace the outsider. To do so may be an important contribution towards preventing them from messing up their lives, and the lives of some innocent victim or victims, by their angry or frustrated overreactions.

Only a few will ever lash out or mess up in some way, of course. But many more who feel, or are made to feel, excluded can sink into a numb existence, harbouring simmering resentments and failing to achieve their potential as unique individuals. People flourish best with encouragement, and within community.

'Why should being alone – in and of itself – be such a matter for derision?' asks the narrator of Margaret Atwood's haunting novel *Moral Disorder*. 'But it was. The alone – the loners – were not to be trusted. They were strange and twisted. Most likely they were psychopaths. They might have a few murdered corpses stowed away in their freezers. They didn't love anyone, and nobody loved them either.'[37]

That nightmare scenario of wild and baseless assumptions is not so far from the waking reality of contemporary conformist culture. We are wary of strangers. At best we greet incomers with indifference, suspicion and barely hidden hostility. We gravitate rather to 'people like us'. At worst, xenophobic groups from the highly secretive Ku Klux Klan in the USA to the neo-Nazi groups of Western Europe intentionally seek to harass or harm people whom they regard as definitely *not* like them.

By not welcoming and seeking to integrate incomers, we miss out on the potential contributions they might otherwise make to us and to others. We are denying, even betraying, their humanity. And by betraying them, we are betraying the God in whose image they are made and who commands us to love our neighbour as ourselves – because he loves them just as much as he loves us. We are, under God, our brothers' keepers.

It is easier said than done, of course. Contemporary 'wisdom' might even counsel the opposite, saying that it is the responsibility of the newcomer to fit in. Certainly there are things that such individuals can do, as we have seen. But the first move should always come from the established group. For the Christian, it's a no-brainer: it is commanded and expected in Scripture.

The ancient Israelites, having been mistreated as slaves in Egypt for several hundred years, were ordered not to 'oppress a foreigner', because 'you yourselves know how it feels to be foreigners'.[38] Put yourself in their shoes, it's saying; remember what it was like; be kind and sympathetic; help them to find their way around. Indeed, the old Israelite rulebook goes further and requires that 'the foreigner residing among you must be treated as your native-born. Love them as yourself.'[39] No discrimination; no relegation to second-class citizenship; in other words, full integration. Welcome them, with open arms.

Such commands are often accompanied with a reminder that God has no favourites. A later psalmist declared that the God who facilitated the development of different cultures by his fashioning of the human psyche 'watches over the foreigner and sustains the fatherless and widow' (that is, the poor of society).[40] If God is concerned and protective, then so should his people be.

Although it is likely that this principle was more ignored than obeyed, it still remains as God's will for his people. Jesus, who was homeless, itinerant and without a regular source of income, was frequently treated to great hospitality. He even instructed people throwing dinner parties not to invite those who could afford to return the favour, but rather those who could not – and he listed as examples the very people whom orthodox Jews of the time would have considered cursed.[41]

In a parable he commended those who quietly fed hungry people, opened their homes to strangers, supplied clothes to the poor, aided sick people, and even visited inmates incarcerated in the crowded, insanitary death-chambers of ancient prisons. These, he says, are the people who will be welcomed into the heavenly realms, rather than those who, preoccupied with their own affairs, remained unmoved by the needs of others less fortunate than themselves.[42]

The early Christians were regularly reminded of the requirement to offer hospitality, and warned not to show partiality in their dealings with others.[43] Yes, it meant trusting people, and running risks. But life itself is a risk, and what we possess is merely on temporary loan. If I have two coats and my neighbour has none, sharing what I have is not a favour but a duty.[44]

That is the mandate. How it is applied will vary according to local circumstances. When I asked some friends about how we might change the culture from defensive insularity to welcoming openness, one senior church leader replied, 'Vision. It has to come from the front.' Politicians, community leaders and church ministers are often so preoccupied with keeping the show on the road that they neglect bigger issues. Jesus tore into the Pharisees for doing that.[45]

The rest of us don't have to wait for good examples and encouragement from leaders, however; we can get on with it ourselves. Just so long as we observe three common-sense rules: don't be pushy (find out first what people really need); don't patronise people who need help; and above all don't offer empty platitudes.

So let's *notice* the wide range of people who fall within any of the four categories of outsider we have noted: incomers, outcasts, loners and the lonely. They exist in every community. Compiling such a list and considering how to meet the needs should be part of any church's or community's mission audit. Among them are:

- Children excluded from school because of behavioural issues perhaps because of domestic, mental health and other background factors.

- Former prisoners whom no one trusts and so they are never given a chance.

- Armed forces veterans struggling to adjust to civilian life.

- People with any form of physical disability.

- People suffering from mental health issues needing long-term, patient support and friendship.

- People with learning difficulties who often enjoy being in community groups.

- Autistic people who lack social skills.

- Shy and retiring people for whom parties are a nightmare but one-to-one friendships are not.

- Teenagers who want a 'good time' but have nowhere to go for it.

- Immigrants and refugees who need help with language, customs, finding work, getting around.

- Romanies and other travellers (they are not all crooks, and there is a strong Romany Christian community).

- People on low incomes (More about that in chapter 5).

- Visitors to church. 'Newcomers will often know within half a second of entering a church building whether they have a chance of joining the congregation'.[46]

- Homeless people (owing to family disputes, mortgage repossessions, unpaid rent evictions, health problems and unemployment – the reasons are many; the remedies are few).

- Older people, especially widows, people with scattered families or mobility problems.

- Single people (please do not let pushy matchmakers near them. Family-orientated churches should provide integrating opportunities).

- Newcomers to your street, area, school or college who need practical help to settle in.

- Refugees from war zones who at the time of writing are finding European doors being slammed in their faces, partly by the fear of residents that our living standards or job opportunities will fall.

But is protecting what we have the highest ethical good? Or is it rather sharing what we have with people who have virtually nothing? If we were in their shoes, what would we hope people would do for us? When my daughter visited a refugee camp in Lebanon for Syrians fleeing from the fighting across the border, a family she met insisted on making her tea.

To do so, someone had to walk two miles to fetch fresh water and then carry it back to the tent, just so that they could show hospitality to a foreign visitor.

It's the same in parts of rural Africa. No matter how poor the family, they will prepare and serve the best food they can for a foreign guest, even if it means they will go short themselves. Normally unemotional Brits return home from such visits tearful and humbled beyond measure.

Generosity and sacrifice take on a whole new meaning after experiences like that. So too do Bible stories, like that of Abraham spotting three travellers and inviting them home for dinner. He selected a succulent calf from his herd (a valuable animal), had it butchered, prepared and served to his guests – while he looked on without eating. Only later did it transpire that he had been showing 'hospitality to angels without knowing it', prompting a New Testament writer to remind his readers to 'not forget to show hospitality to strangers'.[47]

Maybe our stuffy, suspicious culture still has something to learn about kindness to strangers.

Notes

[1] Kim Philby, British spy, *The Sunday Times*, 17 December 1967, quoted by Philip Knightley, *The Second Oldest Profession*, Andre Deutsch, 1986, p.271.

[2] Reported in *The Times*, 3rd October 2015.

[3] John 6:71; 13:26.

[4] Assassins working for Columbian drug barons are today known by a similar Spanish word: *Sicarios*.

[5] A list of the 12 is in Mark 3:16-19. Philip and Nathaniel are identified in John 1:44-45. Matthew's call while Jesus was in Galilee is recorded in Matthew 9:9.

[6] Genesis 2:18.

[7] W. H. Auden, 'Night Mail', *Collected Poems*, Faber and Faber, 1976, p.118.

[8] Daniel Defoe, *Robinson Crusoe*, Penguin Books, 1965, p.202.

[9] Norman Moss, *Klaus Fuchs*, Grafton Books, 1987, pp.13, 20.

[10] Ibid., pp 58f.

[11] Ayaan Hirsi Ali, *Nomad*, Simon & Schuster, 2010, p.39.

[12] Ibid., Introduction, p.xx.

[13] Matthew 7:1.

[14] Mary Shelley, *Frankenstein*, Wordsworth Classics, 1994, pp.104, 161.

[15] The incident was reported in *i*, 24th August 2015.

[16] The story of Cain and Abel is in Genesis 4:1-18.

[17] John Gibson, *Genesis Volume 1*, St Andrew Press, 1981, p.152.

[18] Isaiah 53:2-3; Jesus' refugee status as a child is recounted in Matthew 2:13-23.

[19] Matthew 27:46.

[20] James 2:14-17. Many UK communities have family support groups, night shelters, soup kitchens, food banks, etc. which rely almost entirely on volunteer helpers and funding.

[21] Charles Handy, *The Hungry Spirit*, Arrow Books, 1998, p.86.

[22] John le Carré, *Absolute Friends*, Hodder & Stoughton Coronet Books, 2004, p.198.

[23] Aldous Huxley, *Collected Essays*.

[24] Reported by Tony Paterson, 6th August 2010, www.independent.co.uk.

[25] Natascha Kampusch, *3,096 days*, Penguin Books, 2010, p.120. Later, when a film based on her ordeal was released, she apparently admitted that Priklopil had also repeatedly raped her (*i*, 25th February 2013).

[26] Alan Bullock, *Hitler and Stalin*, HarperCollins, 1991, pp.50, 19f.

[27] Eric Fromm, *The Anatomy of Human Destructiveness*, Jonathan Cape, 1974, pp.406f. Fromm also points out that most political leaders are to some extent narcissistic: 'It may be considered an occupational illness – or asset' (p.202). That may explain why they never seem to listen to the concerns of ordinary people!

[28] Ron Rosenbaum, in *Explaining Hitler* (Macmillan, 1998) argues that Hitler knew exactly what he was doing, and did it deliberately.

[29] *The Times*, 3rd May 2012.

[30] Philip Zimbardo, *The Lucifer Effect*, Rider, 2009, p.252.

[31] Quoted in *The Times Review*, 9th July 2011.

[32] Billie Piper, *Growing Pains*, Hodder and Stoughton, 2006, pp.175, 348. She has since become a successful character actress.

[33] *The Times*, 24th October 2015.

[34] Terry Waite, *Taken on Trust*, Hodder & Stoughton, 1993, p.117.

[35] Richard Foster, *Sanctuary of the Soul*, Hodder & Stoughton, 2011, pp.137f.

[36] Psalm 46:10.

[37] Margaret Atwood, *Moral Disorder*, Bloomsbury Press, 2006, pp.90f.

[38] Exodus 23:9.

[39] Leviticus 19:34.

[40] Psalm 146:9.

[41] Luke 14:12-14

[42] Matthew 25:31-46. The parable echoes the description of true worship (or fasting) in Isaiah 58:6-9.

[43] For example in Romans 12:13; 1 Timothy 3:2; Titus 1:8; James 2:2-4.

[44] Luke 3:10-11.

[45] Matthew 23:23.

[46] Bob Jackson, *Hope for the Church*, Church House Publishing, 2002, p.86.

[47] Genesis 18:1-8; Hebrews 13:2.

Chapter 3
Turn the volume down

Most people need a purpose in life, however vague, if they are to feel that life is worthwhile. But our broad ambitions can develop into restricted drives, drives can become narrow obsessions, and obsessions can lead down blind alleys. We look at how easily our dreams and plans can get out of hand – and how to ensure that they don't.

To themselves, people are usually right.[1]

In an important study of exceptionally gifted young people, Joan Freeman tells the story of Ady. He was introduced to risk-taking in his chaotic childhood home, and later became a compulsive gambler. He 'learned to look forward to the emotional lift that the sweet surge of adrenalin produced'.

Reflecting on his condition, he said, 'I have a general love of excess. It's as though my volume knob has always been stuck in the max position. If something isn't vibrant or dynamic it doesn't hold my interest. This creates a problem because there is no filter in place that allows moderation, although I can choose to avoid something altogether.'[2]

We don't have to be addicted to adrenalin to lapse into obsessive, driven behaviour. Occasionally we come across someone who is 'larger than life', or 'goes too far'. They don't seem to know when to stop, but revel in excess. We ourselves can become so absorbed in work, a hobby or an idea that it completely takes over our lives. We then start to get things out of proportion; we can lose sight of reality. We start to travel the road that leads to suffering and regret.

And there is a strong hint in the New Testament that Judas Iscariot, at least temporarily, was driven by an obsession.

What was he thinking of?

Three main proposals have been put forward to explain what Judas might have been thinking when he approached the authorities with his offer to hand Jesus over. All are heavily conjectural and none is conclusive. But all three suggest that his mind was fixated on a plan which, in the cold light of dawn on the first Good Friday, melted with the mist and sent him tumbling into despair.

Generally, the biblical writers chose their words carefully. For Judas' 'betrayal' they used a common word meaning 'to hand over'. This isn't always clear from English translations which often prefer the shorthand 'betray'. To hand over suggests a considered action, not a sudden burst of anger or rejection.

The first proposal is that Judas had become disillusioned with Jesus' mission. What had begun with great promise was disintegrating into chaos. The disciples mostly thought of Jesus as a political liberator right up to and beyond Jesus' resurrection.[3] Perhaps when Judas realised Jesus was a pacifist spiritual teacher, he threw in the towel and turned Jesus in as a false Messiah, hoping, perhaps, to simply extinguish the Jesus movement.

Intense disappointment can provoke anyone who has believed passionately in a cause to damage or even destroy what they have previously devoted themselves to. From one obsession they turn angrily 180 degrees to its opposite.

The second proposal is that Judas was frustrated with the hostile stand-off between Jesus and the religious authorities. Jesus was highly critical of them, and they of him. But their confrontations usually concerned Jewish religious customs or obscure theology with which they sought to trap him into incriminating himself.[4] Perhaps Judas wanted to set up a proper debate and give Jesus an opportunity to put his case and declare his messianic status in the confines of a scholarly hall.

Tradition (with no biblical basis for or against) suggests that Judas was well educated and connected to the religious elite. If so, he may have become obsessed with the idea of giving Jesus' ministry a helping hand by using his connections. But in doing so, he failed to read correctly the real intentions of the authorities.

The third proposal is that Judas was deeply concerned at the way Jesus kept talking about the likelihood of his own death. To the disciples, it was inconceivable that the Messiah, the long-expected successor to the great king David, should be killed prematurely. Peter had challenged him privately about it without success.[5] They could all see which way the wind was blowing and Thomas seemed convinced that Jesus' proposed journey south to Jerusalem would result in them all being killed.[6]

To prevent an assassination or lynching, Jesus needed to be taken to a safe house for a while, away from his regular haunts, where the crowds wouldn't find him. So Judas got it into his head to take control of the situation and use his connections to make the arrangements.

The novelist Anthony Burgess is better known for his controversial novel *A Clockwork Orange* than for his fictionalised account of Jesus' life, *Man of Nazareth*. But in the latter he imagines the High Priest Caiaphas saying that Jesus 'must be delivered into the hands of his friends – those of his friends, I mean, who are best able to protect him ... even against his will'. Judas agrees and suggests that Jesus' 'worst enemy is himself'.[7] The plot is hatched and the deed is done in the gloom of Gethsemane's olive grove.

Whatever the scenario, Judas realises too late that his obsessive plan is not foolproof. He himself has been revealed as the fool. The betrayer has been betrayed. He has been a pawn in the power games of the mighty. The true intentions of the authorities are not to disprove, debate or detain Jesus, but to kill him. He confronts them in white-hot anger and flings the expenses he had received on the floor (the original word indicates the action of someone smashing something in a temper). In despair, he commits suicide.[8]

We shall never know the truth. All three proposals are plausible. But the common factor in each is that Judas was so obsessed with his interpretation of the situation, so full of his plans to play the hero, that he got it all wrong. That's what happens when obsessions dominate our mental horizons – in Ady's terms, the volume knob gets stuck on max. Obsession for us can have (at least) four dimensions.

Self-belief – convictions and egos

People need stories. From our earliest years we love to hear them, watch them and read them. They help to make sense of our world – where we came from, where we are heading. Our lives are stories still in the making. Key to them and to our personal well-being is having a focus, whether that is providing for our children, changing the world or getting to heaven.

A focused life drives researchers and inventors to find new drugs and create new gadgets. It drives sports stars to sacrifice comfort and leisure to fine-tune their talents and win races or tournaments. It drives others to work hard for promotion or to learn fresh skills. But that sort of personal goal is limited because when it's reached, we need another.

So we also need an all-embracing *raison d'être*, a 'meta-narrative' into which our story fits. A philosophy or set of beliefs can provide a framework on which we build all the intermediate goals and live accordingly. It may be religious or secular, specific or general. For Paul, his meta-narrative was the Jesus story: 'For me, life finds all its meaning in Christ. Death also has its benefits.'[9]

Sometimes a single goal or part of a meta-narrative can become an all-consuming ideology. It's like looking at an object through a telephoto lens. Only the object itself is in focus. The background is blurred and the surroundings are obscured. We call it tunnel vision. It takes over every other consideration, just as it may have done for Judas. Then, life gets out of balance. Then, we're liable to mess up. We become obsessive.

You see it in terrorists and tyrants who are often driven by a passionately held ideology. 'All of us in the Red Brigades [a 1970s para-military group based in Italy] were drug addicts of a particular type, of ideology. A murderous drug, worse than heroin,' confessed one.[10]

A blinkered ideology coupled with a bullish ego drove Josef Stalin, the mid-twentieth century Russian dictator, into mindless violence. Having worked his way up the ranks of the Bolshevik party he set about 'remaking it in his own image' during the 1930s, terrorising millions of his own people along the way. Historian Alan Bullock noted that Stalin was 'convinced that he was the only man with the strength of will to carry through the necessary measures – *provided he was not hampered by the need to pay attention to any other person or institution (such as the party).*'[11]

That conviction of always being right is typical of an obsessive person. Later, during the Second World War, Stalin rejected reports about a build-up of German forces on his border until it was too late and the 'second front' opened up. The reports did not fit his preconceptions, so 'he had the bearers of this information shot as "British spies"'.[12]

The refusal to entertain alternative views has always been the Achilles heel of political leaders and their advisers. Some of the most damning indictments of tunnel vision and the obsessional pursuit of ideological goals regardless of evidence are presented in Tim Weiner's history of the CIA, based on declassified documents and on-the-record interviews with former officers. One report disclosed that in the 1950s' cold war period 'we had constructed for ourselves a picture of the USSR, and whatever happened had to fit into that picture. Intelligence estimators can hardly commit a more abominable sin.'[13] Making facts fit preconceptions is an abominable sin in anyone.

In the Reagan era, the then Director of the CIA, Bill Casey, allegedly rewrote his analysts' conclusions 'to reflect his [own] views'. And under George Bush, CIA Director George Tenet had an 'all-consuming desire to please his superiors' – telling the President what he wanted to hear, in other words. That desire led directly to the infamous report on Iraq's alleged programme of weapons of mass destruction. There was scant evidence for it apart from the testimony of a tortured prisoner and the Iraqi leader Saddam Hussein's proud refusal to admit his *in*capacity.[14]

It's easy to ridicule or despair of tyrants like Stalin or toadies who shore up the egocentric opinions of would-be heroes in the White House, Whitehall or wherever. The fact is we all share the same mental flaws. As psychologist Cordelia Fine explains, our brains filter information like a suspicious border guard whose default attitude to foreigners is 'keep out':

> Evidence that fits in with our beliefs is quickly waved through the mental border control. Counter-evidence, on the other hand, must submit to close interrogation and even then will probably not be allowed in. As a result people can wind up holding their beliefs even more strongly after seeing counter-evidence ... This phenomenon, known as belief polarisation, may help to explain why attempting to disillusion people of their perverse misconceptions is so often futile.[15]

Maybe Messrs Casey and Tenet were on a hiding to nothing. They just valued their meal ticket more than risking dismissal.

It is natural to crave certainty. To maintain it, our ideas, beliefs, even ways of doing things can become obsessions. They give us personal, intellectual and spiritual security. When they are challenged or contradicted, we become defensive. When we're defensive, we're likely to become dismissive.

So if someone in the church challenges a 'traditional' biblical interpretation, all hell can be set loose. They may be accused of not being 'true Christians', of 'departing from the true faith', 'being unscriptural', or 'bowing to modern culture'. Offenders are denounced as traitors, dismissed from organisations or denied platforms they had previously graced. Rapid defensive reactions can shut down considered debate before it has really begun.

It's understandably confusing when such acrimony flares up. People ask in bewilderment, 'Does it really matter? Isn't believing and trusting in Christ enough?' Paradoxically, the answer is 'Yes' to both. Doctrine does matter, enormously. But being *doctrinaire* about some aspect of it risks becoming unhelpfully divisive.

We do need an understandable framework for God's story. There has to be a higher benchmark than personal preference when we delve into the mysteries of eternity. We have to draw the line somewhere between what is evidently true and what is not. A church does need a basis of faith on which its mission is based. We can't truly worship God unless we have some understanding of what he's like. We can't believe and trust in Christ unless we have a clear idea of who he is and why we should bother.

The historic creeds based on the teaching of the Bible define for all time what is authentic Christian belief. However, the creeds are summaries, and to an enquiring mind they raise more questions than they answer. While Scripture amplifies them, the Bible itself is neither a systematic textbook nor a self-help manual. It's when we start to explore the details that disagreements can arise. We all understand and express things slightly differently. While these differences can be like facets of a diamond that make the whole jewel sparkle, sometimes we insist that the glint of our side outshines another.

That's when the devil gets into the detail. The trend in the church, as in society, seems to be of increasing fragmentation. The unity of spirit for which Jesus prayed and the apostles pleaded[16] becomes harder to maintain when the language used is vitriolic and accusatory.

However, this should not discourage anyone from exploring theology. The more we understand about our faith, the greater our reasons for wonder, love and praise. The more we discover about God's purposes, the more we'll be able to live Christianly. God's story as revealed in Scripture is a glorious meta-narrative that helps to make sense of an often dysfunctional and suffering world. We just need to tread carefully along the boundaries between primary unchangeable truths and secondary matters where differences of interpretation or practice are possible.

Note, too, that the manner in which some debates are conducted can have a negative impact on interested observers. The comedian Marcus Brigstocke has admitted, 'I wish I could find a God to believe in.' Such a God, he wrote, is the one 'people describe when they choose to ignore the ugly history of [religion] … I want a God who loves us all in a way that goes beyond words.' What puts him off is that 'religious people will fight about almost anything'.[17]

There is indeed such a loving God revealed in the New Testament, but our ideological obsessions can sometimes hide him from others. We're supposed to love God more than we love argument.

Self-protection – paranoia and fear

Fear is a powerful driver. It's a natural human instinct to protect ourselves, our families and our interests from danger or threat. It's what drives the American gun lobby's insistence on the right to carry arms – to protect oneself from the baddies.

Unfortunately, we can begin to see baddies everywhere. Our lives become ruled by fear and dominated by avoidance strategies. Stalin saw 'fascist spies' everywhere, and arrested millions of people to neutralise the perceived threat. In 1937 he said that 'if just 5 per cent of [them] turned out to be actual enemies, "that would be a good result". Evidence was a minor consideration.'[18] That was little comfort to the 95 per cent who suffered unjustly in labour camps.

Paranoia can grip crowds. During the Second World War there were waves of alarmist accounts of 'fifth columnists', German agents planted in the UK to wage a war of attrition and sabotage. Reports of suspicious people or incidents flooded into the security services, none of which 'led to the discovery of any real fifth column or the detection of a single enemy agent. Fear of fifth columnists, however, produced persistent demands for mass internment from the military authorities.'[19]

A similar public paranoia is emerging today following attacks by jihadists in European cities. Ordinary Muslims who want and have nothing to do with violence report growing hostility being shown towards them. Fear puts individuals on edge and shatters community cohesion. It also breeds pre-emptive violence by vigilantes.

Individually, we can be dominated by a fear of failing, of losing face or status in a group. That sort of fear – a form of paranoia that assumes others have our worst interests at heart – can be crippling. In a laboratory experiment in America, students were asked to do a simple maze puzzle, drawing a line from the centre to the exit without lifting the pencil, to 'guide' a mouse to its hole. Some mazes had a picture of cheese in front of the hole; others had a picture of an owl poised to pounce.

The students were then asked to do an allegedly unrelated test of creativity. British Professor Mark Williams reports, 'Those who'd avoided the owl did 50 per cent *worse* than those who'd helped the mouse find the cheese.' The avoidance 'triggered their minds' "aversion" pathways, leaving them with a lingering sense of fear and an enhanced sense of vigilance and caution. This state of mind both weakened their creativity and reduced their flexibility'.[20]

The more we allow fears to frame our thoughts and actions, the less we are likely to achieve. If not causing us to mess up, they may well prevent us from fulfilling our potential. That in itself is sufficient reason to take to heart St John's assurance that God's 'perfect love drives out fear, because fear has to do with punishment'.[21]

The biblical King Saul was initially a classic example of how God can select a shy but talented person for a significant leadership role. But paralysed by fear, Saul went AWOL at his coronation and hid in the locker room. He recovered and graciously bucked the trend of rulers in those days by refusing to kill those who had opposed his appointment.[22]

Soon, though, he went downhill. Impatient and insecure, he committed the cardinal sin of pride by taking on the role of priest as well as king. He made a rash vow which almost resulted in the death of his much-loved son Jonathan. And when David was secretly anointed as Saul's successor in waiting and began working for him, Saul was consumed by paranoia. He made several attempts to hunt down and kill the fugitive pretender. He turned on his own men, accusing them of conspiring against him, and in a fit of pique slaughtered 85 priests and their families. Not a good advert for monarchy.[23]

By contrast, another timid and potentially fearful biblical figure succeeded in overcoming his handicap. Timothy, Paul's young protégé, was sent to oversee a potentially difficult church in Ephesus. There were powerful voices there advocating false teachings – not variations on the theme of standard Christian concepts but a combination of fanciful 'new age' speculations, Jewish customs and extreme asceticism. Timothy could have been cowed into silence or, like King Saul, descended into self-pity and the conviction that all the world was against him. But instead, with Paul's encouragement, he stood firm against those who reckoned he was too young to know anything. He drew on the spiritual resources available to all: 'For the Spirit God gave us does not make us timid, but gives us power, love and self-discipline.'[24] Or, as St Paul asked rhetorically, 'If God is for us, who can [possibly] be against us?'[25]

Self-confidence – adolescent overkill

Adolescents are renowned for lashing out, breaking boundaries, habitual overstatement and unrealistic idealism. As the realities of education, work and long-term relationships kick in and the raging hormones subside, the passionate exaggeration is usually modified. The idealism may remain, but maturity usually suggests more creative solutions to big issues than blowing the world to bits.

But not always. Add youthful impatience and energy to a strongly held ideology and a paranoid conviction that everyone is against you, and you have an explosive cocktail of passion. Not everyone grows out of it.

Ulrike Meinhof appears to have been such a person. She was the co-leader of the Baader-Meinhof group of urban terrorists in the 1960s and 1970s. They bombed and killed targets mostly in Germany in a self-styled war against capitalism. Having been a professional journalist and vociferous advocate for peace, by her early thirties 'the fervor of her immaturity had not changed except perhaps to grow hotter, the great causes to which she would apply it had changed radically. Not peace, but violence, was now her great good.'

In a study of the group, Jillian Becker concluded that Meinhof 'had long dreamed of personal glory, or having a heroic role to play, since the days of her girlhood in Oldenburg; also, that she had not matured emotionally, so that adolescent extremism, "absolutism," and dogmatic moral idealism continued with her into middle age'.[26] She committed suicide in prison in 1976. She had been driven by her blinkered vision and juvenile impatience into a dead end, when she could have been a creative voice for necessary reform.

Immaturity also led to the catastrophic division of the ancient Israelites. When King Solomon died, he left his stable and prosperous realm to his son Rehoboam. But Solomon's success had been at the expense of imposing a huge tax burden, in goods and forced labour. So leaders, including a former senior civil servant, Jeroboam, approached Rehoboam and asked for a more lenient regime.

The new king consulted his advisers. The old hands advised him to reduce his lavish lifestyle and cut back on the expansionist projects. The young Turks, Rehoboam's friends, anticipating a life of ease at public expense, urged him to *add* to the burdens, and this he duly did. Concern for ordinary people never entered their thinking. Ten of the twelve tribes went off and set up their own less-ambitious kingdom under Jeroboam, leaving the rightful king with a fraction of his father's legacy.[27]

Some people never grow up. The apostles frowned on retarded development. 'Grow up in your salvation, now that you have tasted that the Lord is good,' wrote Peter.[28] Church leaders should help people 'become mature' and grow up into Christ, said Paul – that is, have an active faith that attracts, rather than repels, the interest of others.[29] Such growth is a lifelong process which should promote patient thoughtfulness.

Self-seeking – the intoxication of power

Power is intoxicating. Like alcohol, it reduces a person's inhibitions. Like chocolate, it is intensely moreish. Like some drugs, it both energises the body and bends the mind. It breeds arrogance and a sense of invincibility. It can, in its own eyes, do no wrong. Once obtained, it is very hard to relinquish. Just watch how politicians duck and weave to retain their position.

Power wielded without mercy creates fear, stifles opposition and sows seeds of failure. During Mao Zedong's reign of terror in China, critics were imprisoned or humiliated in enforced public 'confessionals'. Doctors were afraid to diagnose widespread malnutrition – the official line was that there was no famine. Villagers had to hand over their metal tools to be melted down for industry, yet continue to grow crops for export while food shortages at home grew worse. 'No-one dared to say anything. If you said anything, they would beat you up. What could we do?' one survivor asked.[30]

In Mao, all four dimensions of obsession were in play. He was an ideologically committed, paranoid, overconfident and power-crazed leader. He created an impoverished and introverted country which, its fearsome military might notwithstanding, was unable to compete effectively on the international stage of commerce and diplomacy for some years to come.

Everyone secretly enjoys influencing others. We saw in chapter 1 how 'normal' people can be mesmerised by power. In a telling cameo in his novel *David Copperfield*, Charles Dickens has the slimy Uriah Heep say, 'When I was a boy I ate 'umble pie with an appetite. I'm very 'umble at the present moment, Master Copperfield, but I 'ave a little power.' Imagine the relish with which those words were uttered.

Love of power drives bullies in the playground and workplace. It motivates celebrities to dominate vulnerable fans. It tempts politicians and businesspeople to bend truth or falsify expenses. It drives killers and abusers to repeat their foul deeds. It pushes individuals to manipulate others into doing their will in the home, church or community.

Alice Jamieson, who was abused by her father and others as a child, notes, 'The man who hits a woman or abuses a child and gets away with it will grow obsessed with his sense of power and will often come to the disturbing belief that he is above the laws and norms of society.'[31]

Jesus' disciples once debated the power they could expect in his 'kingdom'. Jesus responded unequivocally. Leadership and authority in his kingdom would not be a matter of exercising power but of exemplifying service. 'Those who are regarded as rulers of the Gentiles lord it over them, and their high officials exercise authority over them', he said. '*Not so with you*. Instead, whoever wants to be great among you must be your servant, and whoever wants to be first must be slave of all. For even the Son of Man did not come to be served, but to serve, and to give his life as a ransom for many.'[32] Exerting power does not figure on anyone's spiritual job description.

To emphasise the point at the last supper, Jesus took over the servant's role, washing the disciples' feet in the traditional courtesy offered to honoured guests. He then reminded them, in effect, to abandon the limo, pack away the red carpet, cancel the grand entrance, ignore the curtain call, and instead clean the loos and serve the ice creams.[33] (To be fair, the early church recognised that people should focus on their gifts and talents. They released the apostles from menial tasks so that they could focus on pastoring and teaching, but you get the point – leadership is not about personal gain or public acclaim.[34])

So there we have four dimensions of obsession: What you think, is right (ideology). Look after number one because everyone is against you (paranoia). You deserve it and the world owes it to you, now (adolescent confidence). If you can, do it (power). But so far we've listened to the high volume of obsession. Let's look now for ways to turn it down ourselves, and perhaps help others to do so too.

Look at the big picture

Earlier we saw that being obsessive in any way is like looking at life through a telephoto lens – only the one object is in focus. The antidote, of course, is to change the lens to a wide-angle one, so that we can observe the object in its broader context. Such a view puts things into perspective; the issue may remain important, but we see that there are other equally important matters around it. That may help us deal with our concern more creatively and effectively, and to keep a balance in life and conversation.

Politicians of all parties are fond of appealing to the bigger picture when it suits them. Someone is suffering because they lack bread today? But look how we're ensuring that there will be jam tomorrow. At other times, though, the immediate pressure of maintaining or increasing their share of the vote obscures the bigger picture. Short-termism is the cheap enemy of expensive long-term planning.

Turn the pages of the Bible and you'll find that the stories of nations and individuals only make sense within the context of a very big picture. In the sixth century BC a large number of Judeans were trapped as exiles – prisoners of war – in Babylon as the consequence of previous generations' misdeeds. God, it seemed, had forgotten them.

No, said the prophet Isaiah:

> Lift up your eyes and look to the heavens:
> who created all these?
> He who brings out the starry host one by one
> and calls forth each of them by name.
> Because of his great power and mighty strength,
> not one of them is missing. ...
> [So] why do you say ...
> 'My way is hidden from the Lord;
> my cause is disregarded by my God'?[35]

An unexpected gesture from a new king later gave the Judeans a free ticket home.[36]

When things look bleak, meditating on something like the vastness of the universe can restore vision and hope.

Then there's that puzzling fact that the Old Testament story is so long and convoluted. Why didn't God short-cut to Jesus and avoid all the pain, suffering and slaughter? Paul says Christ came 'when the set time had fully come';[37] that is, God had been setting the scene for the history-changing event. The big epic had been screened and now the sequel (the New Testament and subsequent Christian history), which makes no sense without it, is in production.

And the people caught up in the old? They had glimpses of the new and understood that their walk-on part was contributing to an unimaginably bigger story: 'They were all commended for their faith, yet none of them received what had been promised, since God had planned something better for us so that only together with us would they be made perfect.'[38]

That is probably what St Paul had in mind when he gave the often misused assurance 'that in all things God works for the good of those who love him, who have been called according to his purpose'.[39] There is a big picture. Don't lose sight of it when a bee starts buzzing in your bonnet and proper concern starts to devolve into improper obsession.

Stay humble

Obviously the big picture of anything in modern life, let alone in matters of faith, is so large that we can't hope to see it clearly. '"For my thoughts are not your thoughts, neither are your ways my ways," declares the Lord. "As the heavens are higher than the earth, so are my ways higher than your ways and my thoughts than your thoughts."'[40] Or, in the blunter words of the Bard, 'There are more things in heaven and earth, Horatio, than are dreamt of in your philosophy.'[41]

Bible writers frequently admit the limitations of their understanding. 'My mouth will tell of your righteous deeds, of your saving acts all day long, *though I know not how to relate them all*' declares one psalmist.[42] Another recalls God's complete understanding of human life and concludes, 'Such knowledge is too wonderful for me, too lofty for me to attain.' If he could count God's thoughts, 'they would outnumber the grains of sand'.[43]

Even the great New Testament theologian, St Paul, who clarified many of the cardinal doctrines relating to Christ's death and resurrection, freely admitted, 'For now we see only a reflection as in a mirror; then [in heaven] we shall see face to face. Now I know in part; then I shall know fully, even as I am fully known.'[44] In his day a mirror was just polished brass, giving a fuzzy, pale and often distorted reflection. Today he might have used the analogy of sitting in an arena with a greatly restricted view.

American writer and speaker John Ortberg noted that in matters of faith, 'overconfidence can be a problem. It may sound strange, but some people would be better believers if they had a little more doubt.'[45] We don't know it all, so we shouldn't pretend to. Even Jesus admitted his knowledge was limited.[46]

Former Harvard professor Henri Nouwen, who gave up his job to work among people with learning difficulties, wrote from experience that 'essential for mature religion is the constant willingness to shift gears, to integrate new insights and to revise our positions'.[47]

There's always more to learn – even from those with whom we disagree. Listening to their sincerely held views and the reasons they are persuaded by them can help to put our views into a wider perspective and refine our expression of them, even if we don't change them substantially. What stops us doing that is often the fear that our views will be shown to be less comprehensive and watertight than we think – which is the first step to blind obsession and paranoia.

In Muriel Spark's celebrated novel *The Prime of Miss Jean Brodie*, the young teacher was contrasted with the other school staff. 'She was still in a state of fluctuating development, whereas they had only too understandably not trusted themselves to change their minds, particularly on ethical questions, after the age of twenty. There was nothing Miss Brodie could not yet learn, she boasted of it.'[48]

There's nothing that any of us cannot yet learn. Unfortunately, today's sound-bite culture almost guarantees that we never get to discover the whole truth or see the wider perspective about anything. A short letter to the editor, a 30-second quote or a 140-character tweet can never do justice to the complexities of science, society and spirituality.

We shall return to this later, but meanwhile ponder the experience of American novelist Anne Rice. She abandoned Christian faith in her teens before returning to it in her late fifties. 'In the moment of surrender, I let go of the theological or social questions which had kept me from Him for countless years,' she wrote. 'There was the sense, profound and wordless, that if He knew everything I did not have to know everything, and that, in seeking to know everything, I'd been, all of my life, missing the entire point.'[49]

Our brains cannot comprehend more than a fraction of what the undying creator knows about life, the universe and everything. We can be thankful, though, for the little that has been revealed to us so that we can negotiate an often tortuous path through the maze of human experience. We don't need to know the rest.

Be patient

While God's story continues to unfold over a long period of time, some of the leading characters we meet in that story have their patience sorely tested. God often plays a waiting game.

Only when old Abraham had reached the age when UK citizens today receive a congratulatory card from the Sovereign was his long-promised son and heir born.[50] Young Moses was rescued from infanticide by a canny mother, a cane basket and a compassionate princess because God had a job for him to do. But Moses had to spend the prime of his life as a refugee farm hand before returning to the land of his birth to set God's people free from slavery.[51]

Another former shepherd, David, had to endure some 15 years of pursuit by the paranoid King Saul until his turn came to step on to the throne.[52] In the New Testament, the elderly Simeon seems to have waited much of his life for a glimpse of the promised Messiah. The implication of the text is that after briefly holding the infant Jesus he went happily home to die.[53]

And then there was Saul of Tarsus, the scourge of Christians whose dramatic conversion on the Damascus Road turned him into the champion of Christianity. But not at once. He waited at least 14 years before the call came to set out on the first of his famous missionary journeys.[54]

When Winston Churchill became Britain's inspirational wartime prime minister, he reflected back over his already long life, some of which had been successful, and some of which had been spent in a political and personal wilderness. 'I felt as if I were walking with destiny, and that all my past life had been but a preparation for this hour and this trial,' he wrote afterwards. Although impatient to start, 'I slept soundly and had no need for cheering dreams. Facts are better than dreams.'[55]

We may glimpse distant goals, but it may take years to prepare us for them. We may also be pleasantly surprised, as was Churchill, when an unexpected task is presented to us for which we are now ready.

Patience is not a valued virtue in our time-kept world. We become irritated when the train or bus is five minutes late or when we crawl for ten minutes through roadworks where no one seems to be working. Constantly in touch with the wider world through smartphones and tablets, it is almost too easy to get on our high horse and charge into the latest battle of controversy or criticism. The big picture immediately fades from sight and our adolescent impulsiveness and exaggeration kick back in. Our stress levels rise, until stress becomes a way of life.

Waiting has never been easy, not even in ages past when life generally moved at walking pace. There are notes of frustration in the Bible which have a very modern ring. 'Awake, Lord! Why do you sleep? Rouse yourself! Do not reject us for ever. Why do you hide your face and forget our misery and oppression ... Rise up and help us; redeem us because of your unfailing love.'[56] At least the writer recognised that God's apparent inactivity was not in itself a sign that his love had cooled.

God rarely does instant anything. There is no spiritual equivalent of ready meals or magic wands. Miracles are an exception, not the rule. We need to slow down. 'Wait for the Lord; be strong and take heart and wait for the Lord.'[57] Stick that on your fridge for when you are tempted, as Judas may have been, to throw in the towel or act unwisely.

Be gracious

Novelist Anne Rice, quoted above, reflected on the many conversations about faith that she had witnessed. 'I realize,' she wrote, 'that what drives people away from Christ is the Christian who does not know how to love. A string of cruel words from a Christian can destroy another Christian.'[58]

Or they can simply drive a seeker away. Most of us recoil from harsh and judgemental outbursts, suspicious, perhaps, of the bitterness that seems to lie behind them. Interestingly, the comedian Marcus Brigstocke, having read Richard Dawkins' polemical *The God Delusion* said that he began it as an atheist but 'by the time I finished it I was an agnostic. I was going to read it again but I worried I might turn into a fundamentalist Christian.' What bothered him, he said, 'was the unbearably smug, know-it-all tone of the thing.'[59]

In the Bible passage so often read at weddings, Paul says, 'If I ... can fathom all mysteries and all knowledge ... but do not have love, I am nothing'.[60] Outspoken and direct as he was, Paul recognised that the way in which a debate is conducted or the gospel proclaimed counted as much with God, and the world, as the issue itself.

The Christian elder statesman, the late John Stott, once said, 'It's important to engage with the best arguments of our opponents and not their worst. So rather than creating a man of straw and then destroying it – which is what so-called public debate is so often about – there should be a genuine quest for dialogue and understanding.'[61] That requires patience as well as grace.

We've strayed a long way from Judas, but not from falling into the same trap whenever we sink into any form of obsessive, blinkered thinking or behaving. Bible commentator William Barclay concluded, 'However we look at it, the tragedy of Judas is that he refused to accept Jesus as He was, and tried to make Jesus what he wanted Him to be. It is not Jesus who can be changed by us, but we who must be changed by Jesus … The tragedy of Judas is the tragedy of the man who thought that he knew better than God.'[62]

But that raises another question that has exercised Bible readers for 2,000 years. Did Judas really act on his own initiative? Or did God egg him on? Or even, did the devil take control of him? From dealing with obsession we turn to the dilemmas of choice and responsibility.

Notes

[1] 'Mrs Telman' in Iain Banks, *The Business*, Little, Brown and Co., 1999, p.237.

[2] Joan Freeman, *Gifted Lives*, Routledge, 2010, pp.244-245.

[3] Acts 1:6; cf. Matthew 24:3.

[4] E.g. Matthew 22:15-33; 23:1-32.

[5] Matthew 16:21-28.

[6] John 11:16.

[7] Anthony Burgess, *Man of Nazareth*, McGraw Hill, 1979, pp.278-279.

[8] Matthew 27:5.

[9] Philippians 1:21, New International Readers' Version.

[10] Michael Burleigh, *Blood and Rage*, Harper Press, 2008, p.199; he was quoting an Italian book by Alberto Franceschini.

[11] Alan Bullock, *Hitler and Stalin*, HarperCollins, 1991, pp.515, 514; italics mine.

[12] Orlando Figes, *The Whisperers*, Penguin Books, 2008, p.381.

[13] Abbott Smith, Chief of the CIA Office of National Estimates, quoted by Tim Weiner, *Legacy of Ashes*, Allen Lane, 2007, p.154.

[14] Ibid., pp.379, 487.

[15] Cordelia Fine, *A Mind of its Own*, Icon Books, 2007, p.106.

[16] John 17:20-23; Ephesians 4:2-6.

[17] Marcus Brigstocke, *God Collar*, Bantam Press, 2011, pp.49, 54, 177.

[18] Orlando Figes, *op. cit.*, p.239.

[19] Christopher Andrew, *The Defence of the Realm*, Allen Lane, 2009, p.224.

[20] Mark Williams and Danny Penman, *Mindfulness*, Piatkus, 2011, p.113. The experiment was conducted by others in Maryland University in 2001.

[21] 1 John 4:18.

[22] 1 Samuel 10:20-24; 1 Samuel 11:12-15.

[23] 1 Samuel 13; 14:24-48; 15:28; 22:6-23.

[24] 1 Timothy 4:12; 2 Timothy 1:7.

[25] Romans 8:31.

[26] Jillian Becker, *Hitler's Children*, Michael Joseph, 1977, pp.157f., 282.

[27] 1 Kings 12:1-24.

[28] 1 Peter 2:2-3.

[29] Ephesians 4:11-16.

[30] Frank Dikötter, *Mao's Great Famine*, Bloomsbury, 2010, p.40.

[31] Alice Jamieson with Clifford Thurlow, *Today I'm Alice*, Pan Books, 2009, p.103.

[32] Mark 10:42-45, italics mine; cf. Luke 22:24-27.

[33] John 13:3-17.

[34] Acts 6:1-6; cf. Romans 12:6-8.

[35] Isaiah 40:26-27.

[36] The story is told in the book of Ezra.

[37] Galatians 4:4.

[38] Hebrews 11:39-40.

[39] Romans 8:28.

40 Isaiah 55:8-9.

41 William Shakespeare, *Hamlet*, Act 1, scene 5.

42 Psalm 71:15, italics mine.

43 Psalm 139:6, 18.

44 1 Corinthians 13:12.

45 John Ortberg, *Faith and Doubt*, Zondervan, 2008; quoted in an extract published in *Christianity* magazine, January 2009.

46 Matthew 24:36

47 Henri Nouwen, *Seeds of Hope*, Darton, Longman & Todd, 1989, p.46.

48 Muriel Spark, *The Prime of Miss Jean Brodie*, Penguin Books, 1965, p.43.

49 Anne Rice, *Called Out of Darkness*, Chatto and Windus, 2008, p.183.

50 Genesis 21:5.

51 Exodus 2–3.

52 1 Samuel 16–31.

53 Luke 2:21-35.

54 Galatians 1:13–2:5.

55 Winston Churchill, *Second World War*, 1948, vol. 1, p.526.

56 Psalm 44:23-26.

57 Psalm 27:14.

58 Anne Rice, *op. cit.*, p.227.

59 Marcus Brigstocke, *op. cit.*, p.156.

60 1 Corinthians 13:2.

61 In a personal conversation recalled by Professor John Wyatt and reported by Mark Greene in *Fruitfulness on the Frontline*, IVP, 2014, p.149.

62 William Barclay, *The Gospel of Matthew, Vol. 2*, St Andrew Press, 1958, p.367.

Chapter 4
Did he jump or was he pushed?

Freedom of choice is a prized commodity. It helps us feel we are in control of our life, even our destiny. Yet we can also feel helpless pawns when factors outside our control determine what we do, even who we are. So how free are we, really? Is everything predetermined so that we can do no more than follow a script? Who or what might be pulling our strings? Judas seems to have been subjected to a three-way pull. So are we.

Choosing helps to create our lives. We make choices and in turn are made by them.[1]

The Matrix trilogy of films explores the relationship between people and machines, and the vexed issues of freedom and determinism. When the hero, Neo, enters the Matrix computer program, he is regularly attacked by the dapper, smooth-talking, hard-fighting Mr Smith. His opponent is a personification of determinism and control, and can clone himself into an instant army.

In the third film, *The Matrix Revolutions*, the pair fight yet again and Neo is suffering. 'Why do you keep on?' taunts Smith. 'You can't win. Is it because of some human emotion, like love?'

The breathless but defiant Neo replies, 'It's because I choose to.'[2] That is what makes him human, as opposed to a clever, versatile, manipulative but ultimately impersonal system that cannot choose to be different.

Choice is a much prized and vaunted value. Choice gives us freedom. So long as I have the resources, I can choose what to wear, what to eat, what car to drive. I can choose who my friends are, what sort of job to do, and how to spend my leisure time. My life is not driven solely by necessity or instinct.

However, it's not quite that simple. Choice isn't all it's made out to be. Freedom is not absolute. And what we think are chosen actions can be largely determined by a number of factors. At this point, we enter what wartime Prime Minister Winston Churchill called in a different context 'a riddle wrapped in a mystery inside an enigma'.[3]

The relationship between choice and determinism is a conundrum over which philosophers and theologians have spilled gallons of ink and some blood for centuries. The fact is, as theologian John Wenham wrote, 'Bible doctrine has the remarkable quality of being at one and the same time profoundly mysterious and lucidly clear. At each point there are unfathomable "antinomies" (that is, complementary truths which the human mind cannot reconcile), yet both sides of the picture stand out with intense clarity.'[4]

But it's neither an academic topic to debate nor a mystery we can afford to ignore. It directly affects the way we live and think every day, and is central to our understanding of both Jesus and Judas. What we can do is unravel it enough to discover some important practical truths. We start, not with Judas directly, but with Jesus who chose him.

Director or dictator?

Jesus was born to die. Everyone dies, of course, but Jesus knew from the start of his public ministry that he was destined to be what his forerunner John the Baptist called 'the Lamb of God, who takes away the sin of the world'. Jesus told his disciples that he came 'to give his life as a ransom for many'.[5]

They were alluding to the Old Testament understanding of atonement, that the spiritual consequences of wrongdoing could be eradicated by an innocent victim. Jesus, the unique God-Man, was destined to suffer judicial murder. But he still had a choice. Like an English monarch born to the throne, Jesus the man could have chosen to abdicate (as Edward VIII did in 1936 in order to marry Wallis Simpson).

He grappled with some attractive alternatives to the role of 'suffering servant' in his temptations shortly after his baptism, but he chose to reject them. In the anguish of Gethsemane shortly before his trial, he prayed for a way to avoid the cross, but he chose to stick it out: 'My Father, if it is possible, may this cup be taken from me. Yet not as I will, but as you will.'[6]

He even acknowledged that he could enlist spiritual forces to repel those who came to arrest him. (Some commentators think that was precisely what Judas hoped for: an unmistakeable sign that Jesus was the Messiah.) But he chose not to: 'how then would the Scriptures be fulfilled that say it must happen this way?'[7] From a heavenly observer's point of view, the drama must have been nail-bitingly tense: will he, won't he?

Jesus went to the cross willingly, as a free agent. It had been predicted and planned. But he wasn't forced by his Father. The predictions, which often are much clearer in hindsight than they were when they were uttered, pointed to choices Jesus *would* make. They did not take the decisions out of his hands.

Neither was he forced to select Judas to be among the 12, and nor was Judas a helpless puppet strung along by a scheming God. We've already seen that Jesus on earth did not know everything. He knew early on that someone would betray him, but not the betrayer's identity.[8] It could have been any one of the 12. Jesus did not deliberately choose someone knowing that he would be his nemesis.

Judas had a choice too. Jesus made sure that he got it. During the Passover meal, which the disciples shared before Jesus was arrested, it was customary for the host to offer all his guests a piece of bread dipped in a bowl of herbs and vinegar. To accept the host's offering was a sign of friendship and inclusion. Custom dictated that recipients would not act in a hostile manner against the host.

By then Jesus knew what Judas intended, and through the gesture he gave him a final opportunity to change his mind. A brief conversation ensued between them which meant nothing to the others. When Judas left they just assumed he was going to the shops.[9]

His defection grieved Jesus – another sign that this was the action of a free man. 'The Son of Man will go as it has been decreed,' he said. 'But woe to that man who betrays him!'[10] The word 'woe' is a term of disappointment, not of judgement. It means, 'how sad'. Jesus tried to stop Judas being a fool. Judas chose to ignore the offer. He thought he knew best. And if he had changed his mind? Jesus would still have been crucified; the authorities would have found another way. Judas just made it easier for them.

If we put this into the wider context of the Bible story, two things emerge.

God has plans

Some thinkers in seventeenth-century Europe, called Deists, suggested that God set up the world and then left it and human society to run itself without guidance or interference. This theory finds some expression today among people who believe in a 'supreme being' but don't consider that God has or requires any interaction with us.

The biblical picture is the opposite. God is intimately involved with individuals and corporate groups. Global events and personal experiences occur under his ever-watchful eye. '"I know the plans I have for you," declares the Lord, "plans to prosper you and not to harm you, plans to give you a hope and a future."'[11] That message was sent to mournful Judeans who believed that God had given up on them as they languished in riverside prison camps in Babylon, hundreds of miles from their homeland.

The plan was for them eventually to return to their shattered city of Jerusalem and rebuild it. But as we saw in the previous chapter, God is not quick in fulfilling his plans (it took about 50-70 years in this case). The message therefore also included the instruction to quit moaning, to settle down, to make the most of life abroad, and to let God's plans take their course, slowly. Meanwhile they were to seek the welfare of their adoptive city, and in so doing were assured that they would find their own welfare too.

They also had the words of another, probably earlier, prophet who said, 'Whether you turn to the right or to the left, your ears will hear a voice behind you, saying, "This is the way; walk in it."'[12] God's plan is for people to live responsibly, and to be on constant alert for an often quiet nudge when they stray from God's general direction.

Even in the New Testament, we rarely find the sort of obsession with detailed 'guidance' that bothers many modern Christians. We find Paul using his common sense to plan a mission journey which unspecified circumstances prevented, before a God-given dream suggested another route.[13] It is important to submit our ideas prayerfully to God, but we should not expect a step-by-step list of instructions as if our lives were no more than flat-pack furniture, prefabricated by him for us to assemble.

One way to understand the relationship between God's plans and human freedom is to think of him as the director of a play for which there are only cue cards for key moments, such as the coming of Jesus and his return. The players improvise while the director oversees the broad plot and is available for consultation and support at any time. Just occasionally, he may intervene. 'Although God is in control, he chooses not to exert his control in a way that robs us of freedom.'[14]

We can see this when we look at biblical history. The original creation was a perfect garden. Thrown out of it because of their misdemeanours, Adam's successors built cities, perhaps to afford themselves added security now that they felt (wrongly) that God was rather distant. We have mostly lived in settlements ever since. Move on to the picture of the 'new creation' at the end of the Bible, though, and we find that God has made not a garden but a perfect city (with trees).[15]

It's as if God is saying, 'You chose to develop my world like this. So I'm taking your effort and transforming it into something better. I'm not going to rubbish what you've done.' That is what Paul meant when he wrote that God in Christ purposed 'to reconcile to himself *all things*, whether things on earth or things in heaven, by making peace through his blood, shed on the cross.' God's plan is that we honour him by using responsibly the skills and opportunities he has given. Then we will fulfil his purposes as the 'faithful servants' with differing talents did in Jesus' parable.[16]

It is helpful, too, to recognise that 'time' to us is different than it is to God, as we shall see further in chapter 8. To God, there is no future; our tomorrow is already his today. The author C. S. Lewis expressed this perfectly: God 'does not *foresee* the humans making their free contributions in a future, but *sees* them doing so in His unbounded Now. And obviously to watch a man doing something is not to make him do it.'[17]

People have responsibilities

In the Garden of Eden, Adam was given two responsibilities. One was to look after it; he wasn't told how. The other was to name the animals, and God accepted what he suggested.[18] This is called the 'creation mandate', and it requires the human race in all generations to care for the physical world and its creatures. We are invited to use it creatively, but not to exploit it ruthlessly. But as so often happens, we tend to use our freedom to excess and reap the natural consequences, lamented by a prophet: 'Because of this the land dries up, and all who live in it waste away; the beasts of the field, the birds in the sky and the fish in the sea are swept away.'[19]

Responsibility implies freedom, and freedom gives choice. Cain, later the city builder, sulked when God didn't accept his slapdash offering. God told him to cheer up: 'If you do what is right, will you not be accepted?' God asked. 'But if you do not do what is right, sin is crouching at your door; it desires to have you, but *you must rule over it*.'[20]

That's personal responsibility. Similarly, when the Israelites faced the new challenges and opportunities of entering the Promised Land, they were confronted with an important choice: would they follow God, or their own devices? 'Choose for yourselves this day whom you will serve,' they were ordered.[21] God never forces us to do anything; choice is a gift to humankind to use wisely. It is new every morning.

Finally, there is a lot in Scripture about judgement (whether that is understood as punishment, assessment or appraisal). Judgement presupposes responsibility. We cannot be held to account if we are merely pixels in a Matrix machine manipulated by a divine joystick. That suggests that the contemporary 'blame culture' is a cop-out from facing our responsibilities and, when we make them, our errors. Or, indeed, from recognising that accidents do happen which aren't anyone's fault.

Veteran broadcaster John Humphrys suggests, 'Seeing ourselves as victims means we stop seeing ourselves as responsible'.[22] In the acclaimed novel *The Girl with the Dragon Tattoo*, one character says bluntly, 'I just think that it's pathetic that creeps always have to have someone else to blame.'[23] It's tempting to think that the God who endowed us with choice and responsibility feels similarly.

Sometimes, though, we do become genuine victims when we suffer needlessly through someone else's folly. It can be undeniably difficult to overcome the potentially life-changing effects, but, as many accident victims prove, it is not impossible. At such times we are faced with a stark choice: rebuild our life in a fresh way as far as we are able, or languish in what is called 'learned helplessness'.

Learned helplessness was first noted in the 1960s using laboratory animals in a box. The animals needed to jump a hurdle from one side to another to avoid a mild electric shock. One group had never encountered such a problem but learned in time how to avoid the shock. A second group had had a similar experience before and learned the avoidance technique more quickly. The third group had previously been given mild shocks from which there had been no escape. When these were put in the box, they made no attempt to jump the hurdle. They had learned that they were helpless to change things, so they didn't try.

Since then, other more humane studies have found that people too can 'learn' that they have no control over their circumstances. As a result, they become passive receptors of whatever comes. Professor of social theory, Barry Schwartz, comments that 'learned helplessness can affect future motivation to try. It can affect future ability to detect that you do have control in new situations. It can suppress the activity of the body's immune system, thereby making helpless organisms vulnerable to a wide range of diseases.' He concludes that 'choice enables people to be actively and effectively engaged in the world, with profound *psychological* benefits'.[24]

Learned helplessness is often called 'fatalism', and characterises some non-Christian faiths. It assumes we are trapped inside a pre-programmed universe that we are powerless to affect. Christianity denies it categorically. We were not created, in Paul's words, to be 'tossed back and forth by the waves, and blown here and there by every wind of teaching and by the cunning and craftiness of people in their deceitful scheming'. Rather, we are called to be God's 'fellow workers' in building a better world.[25]

Habits grow from choices

We usually assume that Judas faced a simple alternative: to betray or not to betray. His decision, however, is likely to have been only one in a series of choices that led to it. We have to ask *how* he came to it. He could have considered any one of several possibilities, and each presented him with a choice.

Judas appears to have been secretive and obsessed by his plan, talking to no one. *That* was a wrong choice. He could have aired his doubts or ideas in one of the many exchanges that arose from the disciples' shared confusion about Jesus' intentions and message. Or, he could have discussed them with someone sympathetic but outside the inner group, such as Nicodemus, the Pharisee who questioned Jesus privately in order to understand him better.[26] Seeking other people's perspectives can help clarify our thoughts.

If he was still unhappy, he could have walked away. Others had, when Jesus' teaching seemed to be too narrow or demanding.[27] So was he anxious not to lose face? Was he becoming increasingly frustrated or angry, and instead of managing his feelings he exploded only to regret it later? That was another wrong choice, stemming, perhaps, from stunted emotional intelligence.

Judas could have taken others into his confidence if he was convinced that his plan was the right one. Their support would have strengthened his case. Did the rivalries of the group tempt him to gain Brownie points by going alone, prompted by pride and ambition? Or did he not trust them and feared that one of them would slap him down? Acting from pride or fear is always a wrong choice.

Then there was the money he was given in exchange for information (which we'll consider in the next chapter). That offered him a choice. He could have told Jesus or another disciple that he'd been offered a bribe. The cash exchange might have niggled his conscience and prompted second thoughts. Putting money ahead of morals is always a wrong choice.

Did he stop to ask why the authorities wanted to pay him for volunteering information, or talk to them about *their* plans? If he was trying to set up a meeting, had he taken any steps to produce an agreed agenda for a proper debate? It doesn't seem likely. Being impatient and careless over detail is a wrong choice. Big mistakes are almost always the result of a series of smaller choices that were themselves mistakes, but seemingly inconsequential ones. The slope really is slippery.

One thing leads to another

Early in 2016, Channel 4 broadcast an elaborate stunt by illusionist Derren Brown. It was a modern take on the 1963 'Milgram experiment' at Yale University. In that original, volunteers were told to administer an electric shock to someone in another room whenever that person answered a question incorrectly. After each wrong answer, the shock became stronger. When the victim's distress grew worse the person in charge reassured the volunteer it was OK to continue. Two-thirds of them went on to administer a lethal shock – 450 volts.

What they didn't know was that the victim was an actor and there were no shocks. The point was to show that people will do questionable things if encouraged by an authority figure. Once they began, they were hooked into a course of action that went against their moral code.

Derren Brown's scenario chose a member of the public to take part in a plausible (but staged) high-profile event. The volunteer arrived early and the person in charge enlisted his help to deal with a series of crises. Each involved a moral compromise. The crises and compromises got progressively worse until it seemed that they could only solve their problem by pushing someone off a high roof to his certain death.

At this point, the volunteer on whom the programme focused refused and walked away. 'Good for him,' muttered Derren Brown in the control room. The presenter then revealed that three other volunteers, two women and a man, had been through the same scenario and *had* 'killed' the man. Brief clips of the deed were shown. *That* was the scariest part. Brown had achieved an even higher 'success' rate than Milgram. (The 'victim', of course, was an actor wearing a protective harness.)

How often have we heard someone who has messed up say, 'I had no choice'? Actually, they did – probably earlier in the sequence of events that led to the fateful action. Each time we choose to compromise it becomes easier to do so again, until we're were sucked into an impossible situation.

That is why consistency in everyday life is so important. If we fail to fulfil one responsibility, we'll feel a little less bad about not fulfilling another. If we bend the rules in one place, we're more likely to bend them somewhere else. We convince ourselves that it won't hurt anyone, until eventually it does – and it hurts us too. '*Continue* to work out your salvation with fear and trembling,' urged St Paul.[28]

We hate to admit this, but our moral fibre is surprisingly weak, and our ability to choose is severely limited. That is down to the way our brains work. They are amazingly complex – and annoyingly manipulative. The squishy grey stuff inside our skulls has 100 billion neurons, each capable of interpreting information. They are connected to trillions of synapses, electrochemical pathways which transmit signals to trigger thoughts and actions. No computer has such power (although the Human Brain Project in Switzerland is said to be building a supercomputer that will match it by the early 2020s[29]).

Much of the brain's activity goes on beneath the surface. You don't consciously *choose* to put one leg in front of the other when you walk down the street. Your brain was programmed when you were a toddler to send the right signals to the right places automatically. That frees you up as you stroll to contemplate Einstein's theory of relativity, consider what you're going to say at a meeting, or plan what you'll have for dinner. Every day, we benefit from countless such 'learned responses' or automatic habits.

But they have a down side. The brain works like an internet search engine. Type in 'recipe for pavlova' and in a split second you'll have a choice of recipes plus some adverts for ready-made desserts or glossy cook books. Whenever you search, the engine's algorithms refine the image it has of you so that uncannily relevant adverts or suggestions pop up. Supermarket loyalty cards work the same way, telling the computer to offer extra points or savings on products it 'thinks' you like or need based on your shopping history.

Similarly, everything you do is added to your mental databank. 'You' may forget them; your brain does not. (Although it is a brilliant spin doctor too, and creates a 'story' of our life so far which is always more sympathetic to us than it is to others.) When we encounter a new situation or idea, our internal search engine *interprets* it in the light of what it already knows (or thinks it knows) and offers a response within nanoseconds. It's an interpretation, not an infallible guide. The brain develops habits (including bad ones), determines stereotypes, drives our life into ruts and directs our mind to jump to conclusions. We think we're choosing, but the brain's love of the familiar takes control. It's a mental reflex, called habituation.

Old habits, especially patterns of thinking, die hard. In the early 1990s I was working as a communicator on an inter-church outreach mission in Moscow. Part of the preparation included a meeting for church leaders from across the Soviet Union. At the end, there was a distribution of food parcels – there were still considerable shortages in the country – at the rear of the venue. I needed to see it, in order to report it.

Julia, my translator, and I raced towards the exit stairs which were divided into two sides by a rail. All the delegates were descending down the right-hand side. I led Julia down the empty left-hand side, bypassing the crowd. When we reached the ground she said to me, 'That was a very western thing to do. We would never have thought of doing that.' Russians habitually walked on the right, fearful of arousing the anger of officialdom if they were to step out of line.

Psychology professor and Anglican priest Mark Williams notes that 'habits are frighteningly subtle, yet can be incredibly powerful. Without warning, they can seize control of your life and drive you in a direction totally different from that you'd intended. It's almost as if your mind is in one place and your body in another.'[30]

St Paul knew this from bitter experience. It is exactly what he describes in a passage that has often puzzled readers. 'I do not understand my own actions. For I do not do what I want, but I do the very thing I hate.'[31]

When St Paul visited Athens he met with philosophers on Mars Hill who 'spent their time doing nothing but talking about and listening to the latest ideas'.[32] Nice work if you can get it, but if we don't give real mental effort and time to consider ideas and responses, we could end up pushing someone off a roof. (And don't be misled by the assertion that if you've prayed about it and it still feels right, it is. Our brains are adept at persuading us that we *are* right, and God doesn't always step in and stop us.)

We're not at the mercy of our genes

It used to be believed that our outlook (and hence our actions and reactions) is determined largely either by our nature (our genes which dispose us to think and behave in certain ways) or our nurture (the experiences we have, especially in our early years). Scientists debated which was dominant, although common sense and experience suggested that it had to be both–and.

This is indeed the case, although the science is still evolving, discoveries are still emerging and the arguments still escalating. 'Individual differences in outlook emerge from an ocean of complex and multiple interactions,' says experimental psychologist and neuroscientist Elaine Fox. She explains that 'our environment unleashes or shuts down genes and … genes themselves can affect the kind of environment we experience'.[33]

We're shaped by nature *and* nurture *and* ongoing experiences *and* regular thought processes. The relationship between them all is impossibly complex. While our mental connections tend to run in well-worn channels, like wires in a telephone junction box, grooves on a vinyl record or furrows in a field, thus forming our habits, Professor Fox and others have shown that our neural circuits can be altered permanently.

The brain is malleable; 'plastic' is how the experts describe it. Professor Fox concludes, 'Neurons, and connections of neurons, respond to the things we do and even the things we think, resulting in real changes in the way that brain circuits operate.'[34]

Judas could have altered course, if he'd had a mind too. And so can we, however normal or extreme our life situation is. We can be rewired, make new connections, plough new

115

furrows. We can change our minds. We can break our habits. We can curb our excesses and strengthen our weaknesses. Nasty people can become sweeter. Timid people can become bolder. Aggressive people can become thoughtful and compassionate. If 'neuro-plasticity' can be observed, spiritual 'remoulding' can become a reality, and we'll look at this in chapter 8.

Researchers have also found that the brain can grow. Professor Fox cites tests that showed that the spatial awareness part of the brains of people studying for The Knowledge, the taxi driver's ability to navigate London's 25,000 streets, actually grew in size. She also reports that a Swedish neurologist even discovered in post-mortems of older people who had died of brain cancers that new brain cells had been growing all the time, something that was once thought impossible. Fox concludes, 'The brain never ceases to change and respond.'[35]

The anonymous author of the letter to the Hebrews refers to the deep penetrating action of God's word, 'sharper than any double-edged sword'. We might say, sharper than a surgeon's scalpel or more revealing than an fMRI scanner charting the thinking brain in action. 'It penetrates even to dividing soul and spirit, joints and marrow' – that is, to the very core of a person's being, what J. B. Phillips called 'the innermost intimacies' – and 'it judges the thoughts and attitudes of the heart'.[36]

The writer advocates an intensive focus on the 'solid food' of spiritual truth, like hopeful drivers studying The Knowledge, because 'by constant use [of it, people] have trained themselves to distinguish good from evil'.[37] Perhaps the study of Scripture can help your brain grow!

Too many choices spoil the party

Despite its computing power, the brain can crash. Too much choice confuses it and may paralyse us into inaction, or action we will later regret. This was illustrated when American shoppers were offered six varieties of jam to taste and a dollar-off coupon to buy any one of them. Other shoppers were shown 24 varieties and the coupon. Thirty per cent of those who had viewed the six pots bought one. Only three per cent of those who had viewed the large display bought one. If you think unlimited choice is good, think again.[38] It has even been shown to reduce personal happiness; one secret of well-being is to 'keep it simple'.

Our choices can also be subtly affected by hidden persuaders. Volunteers were given a child custody case study to assess which of two parents would offer the child the best start in life. One group was asked, 'Which parent should have custody?' A majority opted for the wealthier, high-flying parent. The other group was asked, 'Which parent should not have custody?' And a majority opted for the same wealthier, high-flying parent.[39]

The way a question is framed influences our choice. You could say that it *manipulates* our choice. Marketing uses similar techniques to persuade us to buy things we don't really need. We deny it, of course, but just watch the rush for the latest upgrade of a phone or tablet. Are all the old ones broken? Of course not! We've just fallen for the manufacturer's hype (or peer pressure) persuading us that we can't do without the new one even though we've managed fine so far.

So, we do have choice, but it can be distorted without us realising. Judas had choice too. He may have developed some bad thinking habits. But he wasn't forced to act by God. So did the devil push him?

The devil in the detail

Talk of the devil (also called Satan, meaning 'adversary') is unsettling for many people, Christians included. It hasn't been helped by centuries of caricaturing he/it (never she) as an animal-like creature with horns, hooves and a forked tail. Nor has it been helped by occasional media stories of clumsy exorcisms that have gone badly wrong, resulting in the torture or even death of children and adults.

On the other hand, it's not uncommon to hear of celebrities and others talk about 'slaying their demons' after personal battles with anger, addiction, depression, phobias and the like. Politicians haven't hesitated to call terrorist movements 'the axis of evil', and cries of 'evil' erupt from many people's lips when random beheadings, knife attacks and mass shootings are reported.

Sometimes, evil can be palpably real. TV reporter Kate Adie interviewed a police chief in Romania as its brutal regime neared its demise. 'As the police chief came in, the temperature in the room fell like a stone; not as if a door had opened, but as if we'd been transported instantly to a freezing plateau,' she recalled. 'It wasn't a natural cold, of a snowy winter or an icy draught, but a presence of brooding, chilling fear-full evil. Neither Wim [her colleague] nor I are superstitious: but both of us knew that the police chief had been "working downstairs", in the cells, and had brought death up with him.' The interview over, they fled outside.[40]

'Evil' suggests malice, spite, vindictiveness, mindless violence and, above all, inhumanity. We wonder aloud where or what it stems from. In the comfort of our home or the

118

corner of a railway carriage we can't imagine doing such things, but it's just possible, given the right (or rather, wrong) pressure we could be one of the three out of four who push a man off a roof. But that's not evil; that's an error of judgement. Isn't it?

When we do make such an error we try to pass the buck. In a Danish experiment, volunteers had to move an object on a screen. The 'hand' on the screen moved in time with theirs but missed the target. Frustrating, as anyone knows when what you see isn't what you get. They blamed their failures on such causes as magic, hypnosis and outside influences. (But not, it appears, on the computer!)[41]

We're not so far removed from blaming our mistakes on what Paul called 'the ruler of the kingdom of the air, the spirit who is now at work in those who are disobedient' – aka Satan.[42] Which brings us back to Judas; there are three instances when devilish influence is said to have infected him. (Early church and medieval writings made much more of the liaison than the Scriptures.)

At some point (the chronology isn't clear), Jesus acknowledged that one of the 12 'is a devil', identified with hindsight as Judas. Jesus did not mean the devil incarnate had disguised himself as a disciple. Rather, he meant that one of them would become the devil's agent, much as Peter did when he presented Jesus with the tempting thought that he could avoid the cross.[43]

The other biblical associations of Judas with Satan are restricted to two references to Satan 'entering' him. Luke and John both record this but differ over whether it happened before or during the last supper. John also records that Satan put the idea of betrayal into Judas' mind before the meal.[44]

This raises three questions for us. Just who or what is Satan? Did he 'possess' Judas and take control of him? And

119

did Judas have any control over his actions when under the influence of the devil?

The Old Testament knows little of Satan. We meet him in the Garden of Eden manipulating Eve's synapses to make wrong connections. She knows fruit is good. She knows attractive fruit is tasty. So what's the harm in trying this one? Remember, Eve does not know what a lie is. She doesn't know what God means by the 'death' which he warned would result from taking a bite. She is innocent and naive. So she's easy game for a cunning devil. The message is simple: God knows best, so trust him.[45]

Also in the Old Testament there is a reference to Satan inciting King David to hold an unnecessary census; it was a crude appeal to pride in someone who once had propped up the social ladder and now topped it. And there are the exchanges between God and Satan in the opening scenes of the highly stylised book of Job.[46] This is a well-crafted literary exploration of the philosophical and theological problem of suffering based on one man's traumatic experience. It portrays Satan as an accuser, one of the angelic beings intent on frustrating God's purposes and disrupting human life. He's like a snarling Rottweiler on a tether.

It's not until the inter-testamental period, from about 400 BC until the time of Christ, that Jewish thinkers developed an interest in angels and demons. In the gospels we see Jesus casting demons out of troubled souls, and in the epistles there are regular warnings to beware the wiles of the devil and his associates.[47]

Jesus took the reality of Satan seriously. He experienced direct temptations from him and said that his death and resurrection would be a mortal blow to the enemy: 'Now the prince of this world will be driven out.' Satan's final destruction is also previewed in the book of Revelation.[48]

It has become fashionable to suggest that Jesus and the apostles were such children of their time that they attributed to spirits what today we regard as neurological disorders and mental and physical illnesses. But human as he was, with human limitations to his knowledge, Jesus was also divine, and therefore far more spiritually aware than anyone before or since. To him, Satan was real.

But a real what? In one of the few detailed studies of the topic in modern times, popular Bible scholar and evangelist, the late Michael Green, defined Satan as 'an organising intellect, a single focus and fount of evil inspiration ... an intelligence, a power of concentrated and hateful wickedness'.[49] Green demurs from calling Satan 'personal'. Just as God is 'beyond personality', meaning that our personality is but a pale reflection of God's, so Satan is 'below personality', subhuman.

There are biblical hints that Satan 'fell' from heaven, kicked out probably because of pride and a lust for power, taking with him other disaffected spirits. Paul said humans would judge angels,[50] and Satan is a fallen angel. He is not an evil yin to match God's good yang. Not equal and opposite to God. Just a pathetic but crafty loser.

That is not to underestimate this forceful being's power or ability. One of his favourite tricks is to encourage closed minds. 'The god of this age has blinded the minds of unbelievers, so that they cannot see the light of the gospel that displays the glory of Christ,' Paul declared.[51] We've already seen the risks associated with opinions set in concrete. Paul also reminded his readers that Satan's suggestions are very plausible as he 'masquerades as an angel of light' (or enlightenment, even) while being, as Jesus said, 'a liar and the father of lies'.[52] Thoughtful minds open to the Spirit of God are needed to discern truth from error.

So when Satan entered Judas, did he somehow possess him, take over his entire personality, turn him into someone else? There are examples of possession in the gospels, in which people manifest often frightening behaviour. Missionary biographies recount similar occurrences (usually in tribal communities).

Church leaders in the West sometimes encounter situations where forces more malevolent than paranoid schizophrenia, multiple personality disorder and similar psychiatric conditions appear to be at work. Such situations are to be approached with caution and in cooperation with medical professionals. That said, prayer in the name of Jesus can be calming or healing.

Judas was not 'possessed'. He was not 'out of his mind'. He did not act bizarrely; he acted rationally, in a cool, calculating manner. Satan whispered the idea in his head and Judas did Satan's work for him. His mind was made up, and Satan 'entered' him in the sense that Judas became a willing hammer in the hand of the Destroyer (the meaning of another name given to Satan in Revelation 9:11).

Like the legendary Dr Faustus, immortalised in the writings of Goethe and Christopher Marlowe, Judas sold his soul to the devil, willingly. Blinded by his determined passion he blundered on until he realised too late that he had been led by a faulty spiritual satnav up a cul-de-sac with no time to do a U-turn before the road behind him was blocked. You have reached my chosen destination. You're on your own now. Goodbye.

Believe in the devil or not, the fact is that we can be easily led. Jesus' warning to Peter applies to us too: 'Simon, Simon, Satan has desired to sift all of you as wheat. But I have prayed for you, Simon, that your faith may not fail.' We are to 'watch and pray so that [we] will not fall into temptation'.[53]

122

And when temptation comes, there are resources at hand to counter it. 'No temptation has overtaken you [note the powerful verb] except what is common to mankind,' writes Paul. 'And God is faithful; he will not let you be tempted beyond what you can bear. But when you are tempted, he will also provide a way out so that you can endure it.' Or, as James said, 'Resist the devil, and he will flee from you.'[54]

Like an inquisitive, assertive animal, he'll back off if you say boo. Maybe that goat-like caricature has a place, after all. Oddly, one occurrence of the Hebrew word for devil is translated 'goat idols', which were worshipped by Canaanite tribes.[55] It's harder, though, to say boo to the attractive lure of wealth. Money was another factor in Judas' downfall.

Notes

[1] Sheena Iyengar, *The Art of Choosing*, Abacus, 2011, p.268.

[2] *The Matrix Revolutions*, The Wachowski Brothers, 2003.

[3] Winston Churchill, radio talk 1st October 1939, later published in *Into Battle*, 1941, p.131. He was referring to Russia, which had not yet entered the conflict.

[4] John Wenham, *The Goodness of God*, InterVarsity Press, 1974, p.186.

[5] John 1:29; Mark 10:45.

[6] Matthew 4:1-11; 26:36-44.

[7] Matthew 26:54.

[8] John 6:66, 70-71.

[9] Matthew 26:20-30; John 13:18-30. The latter passage may seem to suggest that only Judas was offered the morsel, but this is not borne out by Matthew or normal practice.

[10] Luke 22:22.

[11] Jeremiah 29:11.

[12] Isaiah 30:21.

[13] Acts 16:6-10.

[14] Krish Kandiah, *Paradoxology*, Hodder & Stoughton, 2014, p.237.

[15] Genesis 4:17; Revelation 21.

[16] Colossians 1:20, italics mine; Matthew 25:14-30.

[17] C. S. Lewis, *The Screwtape Letters*, Geoffrey Bles, 1961, p.121.

[18] Genesis 2:15, 19-20.

[19] Hosea 4:3.

[20] Genesis 4:3-12, italics mine.

[21] Joshua 24:15.

[22] John Humphrys, *Devil's Advocate*, Hutchinson, 1999, p.11.

[23] Stieg Larsson, *The Girl with the Dragon Tattoo*, MacLehose, 2008, p.425.

[24] Barry Schwartz, *The Paradox of Choice*, New York: HarperCollins, 2004, p.103. He describes the animal experiment on p.102.

[25] Ephesians 4:14; 1 Corinthians 3:9. Paul is referring here to church growth and mission, but the principle applies more widely, as evidenced by the creation mandate noted above.

[26] John 3:1-15.

[27] John 6:60-71.

[28] Philippians 2:12, italics mine.

[29] *The Times*, 2nd March 2013.

[30] Mark Williams and Danny Penman, *Mindfulness*, Piatkus, 2011, p.68.

[31] Romans 7:15 (New Revised Standard Version).

[32] Acts 17:16-21.

[33] Elaine Fox, *Rainy Brain, Sunny Brain*, William Heinemann, 2012, p.96.

[34] Ibid., p.127.

[35] Ibid., pp.128, 139.

[36] Hebrews 4:12.

[37] Hebrews 5:14.

[38] Barry Schwartz, *op. cit.*, p.21.

[39] Cordelia Fine, *A Mind of Its Own*, Icon Books, 2007, pp.80f.

[40] Kate Adie, *The Kindness of Strangers*, Headline, 2005, p.251.

[41] Cordelia Fine, *op. cit.*, p.100.

[42] Ephesians 2:2.

[43] John 6:70; Matthew 16:23.

[44] Luke 22:3; John 13:2, 27.

[45] Genesis 3.

[46] 1 Chronicles 21; Job 1–2.

[47] For example, Luke 8:26-39; Ephesians 6:11-12; 1 Peter 5:8-9.

[48] Matthew 4:1-11; John 12:31; cf. John 16:11. Revelation 5:11-14 and 20:10 offer glimpses of spiritual beings in God's realm and the final destruction of the devil, for which also see Matthew 25:41.

[49] Michael Green, *I Believe in Satan's Downfall*, Hodder & Stoughton, 1981, p.30.

[50] For example, Luke 10:18; Revelation 12:7-9; 1 Corinthians 6:3.

[51] 2 Corinthians 4:4.

[52] 2 Corinthians 11:14-15; John 8:44.

[53] Luke 22:31-32; Matthew 26:41.

[54] 1 Corinthians 10:13; James 4:7.

[55] Leviticus 17:7.

Chapter 5
The lure of wealth

'The love of money is the root of all kinds of evil' is a well-known biblical saying. When Judas betrayed Jesus he was given money for his effort. Ever since, the magnetic attraction of wealth has drawn people into all kinds of trouble. In this chapter we examine why this might be, how to regard and use our resources more creatively, and what might be done for those who lack them.

Under capitalism man exploits man. Under communism it is the other way round.[1]

Apart from a few blips, it had been the best of times. Suddenly, it became the worst of times. The world as many people had known it for half a century ended in September 2008. The respected investment bank Lehmann Brothers collapsed, and if it hadn't been for massive government bailouts on both sides of the Atlantic, others would have followed it like a line of falling dominoes.

Holes in the world economy had already appeared the year before when Fannie Mae and Freddie Mac got into trouble. These American mortgage lenders (their odd names came from the initials of their official titles) had offered credit to thousands of people who had no realistic hope of repaying them. They had to be nationalised to save them.

In the murky world of the sub-prime housing market and the even murkier world of international financial trading, toxic loans were packaged together and sold on to other firms. It soon became apparent that these 'products' were barely worth the paper they were written on. Financial institutions were playing a deadly game of pass the parcel, and when the sweet music of tinkling profits stopped, they found themselves holding a bomb that threatened to blow them to bits.

The world panicked. In Britain, investors formed long queues to withdraw their money from the crumbling Northern Rock Building Society before the government shored it up. The global economy crashed. Investment, output and consumer spending plummeted. Property values fell. Companies went bankrupt. People lost their jobs and homes.

Only in Iceland were some of the architects of the downfall jailed for antisocial and negligent practices. Elsewhere a few top executives resigned with large pay-offs or pensions. Regulators tinkered with the system but didn't change it wholesale. Apart from receiving reduced bonuses, most of the people responsible were left, pun intended, to laugh all the way to the bank. Business slowly returned to normal.

'Normal', though, is not the same for everyone. On 'Black Monday' in 1987 when the American stock market crashed, journalist John Cassidy visited a watering hole on Wall Street frequented by city traders. He found them in buoyant mood. While millions of dollars had been wiped off the values of big companies, leaving shareholders facing huge losses, the traders had made a mint selling stocks. 'The interests of financial insiders often differ from those of regular investors,' he reflected.[2]

Money can distort our view of reality, morality and social responsibility. The pursuit of possessions can act like a moral and spiritual blindfold. It can cause personal and communal suffering. This is nothing new. It seems that Judas was caught by the lure of money, and trapped into betraying Jesus.

Exactly how money influenced Judas' action is unclear. Two of the four gospels record a deal between him and the chief priests. Matthew, who alone mentions 30 pieces of silver, says that Judas specifically asked, 'What are you willing to give me if I deliver him over to you?' Luke, who claimed to be a careful historian (Matthew had another, theological, agenda) is more guarded. He says that Judas went to the priests to discuss 'how he might betray Jesus'. Delighted, they 'agreed to give him money' to which 'he consented'.[3]

That could mean that they offered him a gift for his trouble. It could also mean that there was some typical middle-eastern haggling in the discussion. John's gospel reveals that Judas was the treasurer for Jesus and the apostles. He also had his hand in the till (although that did not become evident until after his death).[4] He probably had a weakness for money. So do many of us.

The hidden cost of human exploitation

According to ancient Israelite law, the fee of 30 silver pieces was the compensation (or redemption fee) paid to a slave owner if the slave was killed by another person's animal. It also appears to have been a standard cost of a slave, and regarded as a relatively insignificant sum to seal a contract.[5]

The symbolism is significant. Jesus 'belonged' to neither Judas nor the priests yet they regarded him as a commodity to be traded. Slavery is the ultimate expression of dehumanising someone, of taking full control of their life. In selling Jesus, Judas was asserting his power over his former friend. He was trying to hurt him, or force him to conform to his own plans.

Slavery was endemic in the ancient world. Israelite law forbade enslaving fellow Hebrews except as payment for serious debt. Those slaves were to be freed after six years and given the means to become self-sufficient once again.[6] The law was less generous to foreign slaves, although they were entitled to a day off each week and to participate in Israelite festivals.[7]

So common was slavery that Paul used the imagery of 'redeeming' slaves to illustrate his theology of Christ's death. 'You are not your own; you were bought at a price', he wrote. Christ, who in effect became a slave, set us free from slavery to sin (that is self-centredness) to become 'slaves to righteousness' in a willing response of love and service to God.[8] Jesus himself used similar imagery when he spoke of being 'a ransom for many', a term still used today in relation to payments for the return of hostages.[9]

Jesus, who having been sold as a slave went quietly to his execution, never spoke about the system of slavery. There is one New Testament reference that condemns slave *traders*, lumping them with 'the unholy and irreligious … murderers … the sexually immoral … liars and perjurers' as 'lawbreakers and rebels'.[10]

Had the early church openly opposed slavery it would have attracted additional persecution to its tiny, fragile congregations that in any case comprised both slaves and owners. Christians were already struggling with religious and cultural opposition from both Jews and Romans. The church as an influential or campaigning institution did not yet exist.

However, the apostles did begin to undermine the institution. Masters and slaves were told to treat each other with respect and kindness as human beings equally loved and redeemed by Christ. This set a standard for employment relations in all periods of history. When Philemon, a runaway slave, became a Christian through Paul's preaching, the apostle sent him back to his Christian owner Onesimus. But he also asked Onesimus to treat Philemon as a brother and to release him so that he could work with Paul.[11]

It took almost two millennia for the slave trade to be officially abolished in 1807, largely through the persistence of Christian politician William Wilberforce in the UK and the Quakers in the US. That was followed in 1833 by the Emancipation Act which abolished slavery altogether.

Yet it still goes on. Human trafficking is said to be the second most profitable crime in the world, worth $32 billion. Only the drugs trade earns more black money. Today there are believed to be some 36 million slaves in the world, trafficked into sweatshops, prostitution and military groups.[12]

Respect and kindness, dignity and freedom are the least any human being should expect to receive from another. Part of Jesus' mission was 'to release the oppressed', and that does not refer just to personal spiritual bondage unrelated to physical circumstances. He was echoing the call for social justice made by the prophets before him.[13]

Yet far from the criminal world of people trafficking, we can still trample on people's dignity and restrict their freedom. Our continued demand for cheap goods reinforces oppression in faraway sweatshops. The savings we make (to spend on more things) are our equivalent of Judas' 30 pieces of silver, our reward for condemning the innocent to slavery. Fair trade deals and campaigns to monitor how products are made are but a small step towards justice. There is still a long way to go.

Although exploitation is outlawed, we are not entirely free from the mental attitude that treats people in less than dignified ways. In the UK, zero-hours contracts (forced on about a million people) offer contracted workers no guaranteed income. For people who just want occasional work and are able to be flexible, they're fine, but not for families dependent on a regular income but who can find no other work.

Staff were once called 'personnel', meaning 'the body of persons engaged in any service or employment' according to *The Shorter Oxford Dictionary*. Now, though, they are 'human resources'. A resource is something expendable, essential for a task but bought as cheaply as possible to maximise profits.

But people are not merely units of production. They are partners in a process. They are assets to be valued and cared for. Companies that take staff welfare seriously, managers who take an interest in their workers' whole-life experience, firms that are sympathetic to parents' needs for flexibility: these generally have happier workplaces, with more creative and cooperative staff, and are no less profitable.

Like Judas, we can suffer from defective moral vision, failing to notice (or care about) the spiritual and social consequences of our drive for wealth or profit. Jesus came not only to release the oppressed; he came also to bring 'recovery of sight to the blind'. Judas was driven to sell Jesus by his blind obsession. The priests were blind to justice, eager to purchase Jesus in order to preserve their power and status. They have successors today.

The darkness of corruption

The priests' payment to Judas had a second effect. They didn't just buy Jesus; they bought Judas. He became *their* slave.

If he failed to deliver, or ran off with the money, they could expose and shame him. They knew where to find him. They could send in the heavy mob to ensure that he kept his side of the deal; they clearly had one, judging from the crowd who came to arrest Jesus and those who shamelessly made false statements in Jesus' trial. They could torture or kill Judas – he was expendable.

From that point, like some of the people we saw in chapter 1 who were coerced into doing bad things, Judas probably felt he had no choice, even if he wanted one. He was trapped. He was doomed if he handed Jesus over, and damned if he didn't. The money was a bribe. The deal was corrupt. Judas wasn't in control; the priests were.

Such 'buying' of people is standard practice for controlling double agents. Former Director of the American intelligence service, the CIA, Richard Helms, stated in a testimony to the US Senate, 'You can't count on the honesty of your agent to do exactly what you want or to report accurately unless you own him body and soul.'[14]

The eminent scientist Klaus Fuchs handed British and American atom bomb secrets to the Russians in the 1940s. When he restarted his shady career after a pause, he accepted £100 from his Soviet handler. 'He took the money as an assurance of his commitment and loyalty, after being out of contact for a time,' comments his biographer. 'For someone as independent as Fuchs, accepting the money was a gesture of humility, a bending of the knee.' He had been bought.[15]

Corruption, like slavery, is as old as the human race. In ancient times merchants would use two sets of weights: a

132

light set for buying and a heavy set for selling. With one, they got more product for their money. With the other, they got more money for their product. 'The Lord your God detests anyone who ... deals dishonestly,' the Israelite law stated. The prophet Amos condemned merchants who were 'skimping on the measure, boosting the price and cheating with dishonest scales ... selling even the sweepings with the wheat'.[16]

The biblical standard was clear: 'Do not pervert justice or show partiality. Do not accept a bribe, for a bribe blinds the eyes of the wise and twists the words of the innocent. Follow justice and justice alone, so that you may live.'[17]

The lure of easy money can be irresistible. Corruption is a deep hole to fall into and very hard to climb out of. Sometimes it is cleverly disguised, like an animal trap in woodland. It can snare anyone, church members included. 'If you think you are standing firm, be careful that you don't fall!' Paul warned.[18]

To take a backhander or grease someone's palm, however innocuous it seems, is to play with fire and risk getting burned. It ties both recipient and giver to each other. They are partners in crime. They have ceased to 'walk in the light' as John called the lifestyle God intended people to follow.[19] They have entered the darkness of the underworld.

So too has the person who skims off money or property from an organisation, or inflates their expenses. Managers may not notice it; we may even think they owe it to us, but it singes our conscience, distorts our values and weakens our resolve. It will be easier to do it again. And again. Until we're caught. If we're really on the breadline, we need to seek help, not help ourselves on the sly.

In international trade, payments to middlemen are often taken for granted. In the West, consultants can charge high fees for doing very little. It's legal but it inflates the price of the work or product, and costs customers more. One person's illegitimate gain is another's inevitable loss. Taking a stand against this is hard, and can cost contracts, even jobs. But if corruption is to be defeated, righteousness must reign.

Corruption affects the whole community. In the year ending September 2015, Financial Fraud Action UK reported 1.4 million cases of card, cheque and remote banking fraud in England and Wales. Credit card scams were reckoned to cost the UK about £30 billion annually.

Some of the huge commercial scandals over the past quarter-century have cost ordinary people dearly. In one example, Allen Stanford, a tycoon who had sponsored international cricket's Twenty20 competitions, was sentenced in 2012 to life in jail for defrauding 28,000 victims to the tune of £4.5 billion, much of which had furnished his lavish lifestyle. Many victims lost their life savings in his 'Ponzi' scheme which offered investors high returns based on false statements.

Theft (which is what fraud is) isn't just a matter of personal wrongdoing. Paul puts it squarely into the context of social responsibility. He quotes four of the Ten Commandments, including 'You shall not steal' and 'You shall not covet', and says that they are summed up in the rule, 'Love your neighbour as yourself.' He adds, 'Love does no harm to a neighbour.'[20] But corruption does; it intends to.

Corruption seeks to buy privilege or power that it has no right to. A sorcerer named Simon saw how the Holy Spirit transformed people to whom the apostles Peter and John ministered. He offered money to learn for himself what he assumed was clever magic. 'May your money perish with you, because you thought you could buy the gift of God with money!' Peter responded. 'You have no part or share in this ministry, because your heart is not right before God.'[21]

This was conveniently overlooked in the Middle Ages when 'simony' was rife. In Germany, Albert of Brandenburg held two bishoprics (despite not being old enough to be ordained). He also wanted to be Archbishop of Mainz, to give him authority over the entire German church. He negotiated a fee to buy the office (the Pope badly needed the money). Albert borrowed it from a bank and obtained Pope Leo X's permission to sell 'indulgences' to repay the debt. Indulgences were spiritually worthless promises of a short cut to heaven. They were a fundraising scam which the public bought in good faith until Martin Luther rediscovered the biblical message that eternal salvation is a free gift from God, and the sixteenth-century reformation began. God is not a vending machine dispensing grace in return for a donation to the church. Would-be benefactors take note.

That's why Jesus overturned the tables of the traders in the Temple in one of his few recorded outbursts of righteous anger. They were profiting (often excessively) by turning the worship of God into a financial transaction.[22]

Today, some shady practices come close to being corrupt 'in spirit' even if they are strictly legal in practice. Offshore holdings, and accounting procedures that avoid paying taxes to the country in which profits are earned, are among them. Another is the practice of large organisations to fund research which presents a favourable picture of their activities but which is questioned by less well-funded independent analysts. Some give senior civil servants corporate hospitality at prestigious events; others make large donations to political parties. How can even an impartial official reward such 'friendship' with higher tax demands or restrictive legislation?

American behavioural economist Dan Ariely gave up doing consulting work and expert witness testimony. 'He

135

knows from research that if he is paid by a company it is almost impossible not to see reality from their perspective,' commented feature writer Rachel Carlyle.[23]

Corruption and shady dealing rightly anger us, so Jesus' approach to the corrupt tax collector Zacchaeus is instructive. He did not curse him, nor demand that he reform himself. He simply offered him friendship. Zacchaeus knew that he had broken God's rules and therefore assumed that God had no interest in him. On the contrary, Jesus said, 'The Son of Man came to seek and to save what was lost.' Zacchaeus accepted the invitation and then sorted himself out, by repaying more to those he had defrauded than even the compensation law required.[24] He had discovered that he was loved and accepted by God. Only then did he see how devastating his actions had been to others. A weakness of modern law is that the compensation given to victims is often inadequate.

Similarly, Paul anticipates a crook's changed priorities: 'Anyone who has been stealing must steal no longer, but must work … that they may have something to share with those in need.'[25] This is not to deny that criminals should be punished in law; rather it is a promise of spiritual hope for repentant fraudsters who convert their misdirected talents into beneficial activities.

However, on one occasion Jesus appeared to commend a corrupt manager who faced the sack because he was wasting his boss's resources. Knowing he needed a new job, he called his boss's creditors and marked down their debts in the hope that they might repay him with work. The boss actually commended him for his shrewdness despite the fact that he had been robbed.

In his explanation of the story, Jesus labelled the manager dishonest, but went on to say that if we have resources, we should consider how to use them (honestly) to make friends and influence people *not for our own benefit but to draw them towards God's kingdom*.[26] Wealth is for utilising, not hoarding.

The desire that is never satisfied

The most common assumption about Judas' betrayal of Jesus for 30 pieces of silver is that he was just plain greedy. He wanted money, which is perhaps why he dipped into the common purse. 'Whoever loves money never has enough,' observed a wise man centuries before Christ. 'Whoever loves wealth is never satisfied with their income. This too is meaningless.'[27] It is, but hard to accept and an even harder temptation to resist.

Bernie Madoff, sentenced to life imprisonment for a multi-million pound fraud he ran in the 1970s and 1980s, found money rolling in as a result of his false reports of massive profits on his non-existent investments. 'It is a head trip,' he told journalist Steve Fishman in a prison interview. He couldn't resist carrying on, it was exciting, until the bubble burst and he, like his investors, lost everything.[28]

'Greed' is not a word we might use of ourselves, but 'desire' is. As our lifestyles have improved, so have our aspirations. 'You're paid a lot and you're not happy, so the first thing you do is buy stuff that you don't want or need – for which you need more money' was the acute observation of novelist Douglas Adams.[29]

As money increases, so, it seems, does meanness. A Church of England survey in 2014 found that churchgoers earning £10,000 or less gave proportionately more than people on £40,000. People in poorer areas of the country gave proportionately more than those living in richer areas.[30]

Paul Getty, who at the time of his death in 1976 was said to be the world's richest person, 'became a legend for his miserly attitudes: he kept a payphone for his guests in his country house ... and he left behind him a legacy of bitter disputes and resentments among his children, of whom he had seen little.'[31]

And with meanness grows indifference. Jordan Belfort, the multimillionaire 'wolf of Wall Street' who was jailed in 2002 for a \$100 million fraud, wrote that his life had become 'all about excess: about crossing forbidden lines, about doing things you thought you'd never do'. Driving through a wealthy (but not opulent) area, he reflected, 'It was rather ironic how a kid from a poor family could become desensitized to the extravagancies of wealth to the point that million-dollar homes now seemed like shacks.'[32]

Was that Judas? Was he tired of tramping the country, living hand to mouth and camping under the stars with a bunch of northern artisans, using the money he pilfered and the payment from the priests to buy himself a few treats? Or was he building up a bit of capital for when the dream of the Jesus revolution burst, as it surely would after his betrayal, so that he could take up his old life again?

Perhaps. People who have little can grow resentful of those who have more; covetousness is only a short step from corruption. Being denied by circumstance of what others take for granted can be depressing, and depression can cause someone to snap, and grab.

The hunger factor

Judas could have been hungry, literally. Only people who have had to watch others indulge while they go without will know what this feels like. Seeing others enjoy meals out, leisure trips and holidays when there is barely enough in the kitty for a few items from a supermarket basics range can be galling for people on low incomes. There are many of them,

138

hidden below the radar of TV documentaries and glossy magazines.

We know of two occasions when Jesus and the apostles were hungry. Once they were walking through cornfields plucking (gleaning) grain, eating it raw. The practice was allowed in Israelite law. On another occasion, they passed a roadside fig tree and found it frustratingly barren, probably because it was diseased. The fact that Jesus cursed it, and used its subsequent withering as an illustration of both faith and judgement, takes nothing away from the fact that he needed food.[33]

Modern law forbids gleaning and prosecutes shoplifters. Technically, even bin-surfers are guilty of theft, although supermarkets are unlikely to press charges when scavengers help themselves to food past its 'best before' date in the shop's skip. But desperate people will risk anything to eat and feed their families. They may mess up by getting a criminal record. Yet perhaps it's the rest of us who have messed up by contributing to a situation in which beggars cannot be choosers and may become thieves.

The debt factor

Perhaps Judas was in debt. There were no bankruptcy or debt reduction schemes in his day. The Old Testament law did have the Jubilee principle for the return of money and the cancellation of debt, but that only operated once every 50 years, and it may not have been widely observed even then.[34]

Moneylenders were private individuals, a bit like payday loan sharks today, who could be ruthless in pursuit of money (and interest) owed to them. Jesus told a parable about someone who was let off a big debt but who then had one of his creditors thrown into prison for not repaying a much smaller sum. Nasty.[35]

139

Massive debt led to the 2008 financial crash. It was not just private debt in mortgages and on credit cards, but the eye-watering sums financial institutions were borrowing from each other on the merry-go-round of trading obscure options, derivatives and similar products.

Jesus issued a warning about getting into debt: 'Settle matters quickly with your adversary who is taking you to court,' he said. If not, you will be imprisoned and 'will not get out until you have paid the last penny' – a catch-22 situation because once in prison there was no possibility of earning the money.[36] That's not far from where many people find themselves today; clearing debts is fiendishly difficult.

The gambling factor

A passion play put on in Amiens Cathedral in northern France depicted Judas as a regular at the local casino.[37] Fanciful, perhaps, but gambling is a massive Judas trap. In the financial markets, many of the 'trades' are simply sophisticated bets on the future prices of stocks or commodities. This came to light in the first case of a modern bank crash. Senior managers of the venerable Barings Bank didn't understand the complicated deals their star trader Nick Leeson was making, but they were content to let him trade with the bank's money while the profits were rolling in.

But then the profits turned to losses. Leeson's big bets on movements in the Japanese stock market failed. He had not hedged them with counter-bets as insurance. Barings lost a billion dollars, twice its available capital, and became insolvent. Leeson left a note on his desk before attempting to flee justice: 'I'm sorry.' He was jailed in Singapore for six years in 1995.

Risk-taking is still part of the financial culture. In 2012 another star trader, Kweku Adoboli, working for the global investment bank UBS, was jailed for seven years for running a £1.4 billion fraud. It had relied on spread-betting, a particularly risky activity that gambled on changes in the prices of shares. The court case and media investigations revealed that a gambling culture among traders extended far beyond their work: they would gamble on anything, it was said.

It is deeply worrying that the much-desired growth in the world economy is at least partly dependent on people gambling vast sums on future trends. 'The world economy has been taken to the brink by a mania for speculation,' said the authors of an analysis of the 2008 crash.[38] Jesus' parable about the man who built his house on sand, which fell during a storm, offers an uncomfortable parallel to the reality of the money markets.[39]

The financial crash was a huge betrayal by the people to whom, by default, we had entrusted the stability of the world economy. The financiers whose primary purpose was to oil the wheels of trade and commerce abandoned their responsibility and gambled other people's money in the hope of reaping rich rewards for themselves.

The Bible says little about gambling. Christians differ over the ethics of gambling but generally are cautious about both the highly addictive nature of it and the likely waste of God-given resources abandoned to chance. The odds are always in the favour of the bookie and the lottery organiser. Careers and families have been destroyed by gambling, their long-term well-being betrayed by the gambler's forlorn hope of amassing easy money.

The anger factor

Maybe Judas wasn't in debt, to gambling or anything else, nor impoverished and hungry. He could have been angry. Just before he went to the authorities he had witnessed Jesus' friend Mary (the sister of Lazarus, who Jesus had raised from the dead) empty a jar of expensive oil of nard over Jesus.

It was an extravagant act of love and devotion. Nard was used for embalming corpses, and Jesus defended her action, saying that she had prepared him symbolically for his impending death. The disciples were outraged at the apparent waste, and complained that the oil could have been sold and the money given to the poor. In one gospel account, Judas is named as the complainant; in another, they all seem to have agreed. Perhaps he was the one who merely voiced what they were all thinking.[40]

If Judas was angered by Jesus' talk about death, or was frustrated by the spiritual rather than social and political focus of Jesus' ministry, this could have been the last straw. He exploded. He'd had enough. This wasn't what he'd signed up to. He went to the authorities with a plan, and the money then came as a bonus. How could Jesus possibly lead a popular uprising if he accepted such an indulgence?

That, of course, has long been a complaint against politicians, businessmen and even church leaders who declare themselves the people's friend and then luxuriate in the trappings of office. It didn't apply to Jesus, but the attraction of luxury as a reward for a successful struggle or strategy is always strong.

We may not be greedy, we may not gamble, we may not feel jealous of people who have more than we do, yet life still revolves around acquiring and using wealth and possessions. To some extent it has to – we have to make ends meet. Almost without realising it, money changes from being a good to being a god.

The god of this world

Jesus once said, 'You cannot serve both God and Money [mammon].'[41] There is no known god by that name in the pantheons of the ancient world, and it seems unlikely that Jesus was referring to a specific demonic being. He never otherwise personified specific sins or evils. (The sixteenth-century poet John Milton refers to Mammon as a fallen angel who had always eyed heaven's gold rather than heaven's God.)

Jesus was highlighting what people in every generation have known: that wealth and possessions acquire a god-like status and can exert a demon-like influence over us. What we own comes to own us. Just think how hard it is to downsize or take a pay cut when moving to a 'more worthwhile' job.

Today, mammon, parading under its alternative name of 'the economy', rules the world. Political policies and decisions defer to it. Early in 2016 Japan began offering 'negative interest' – charging people to save money so that instead they would spend all they had to boost the flagging economy. A 2016 campaign claimed that extending UK Sunday trading laws would boost the economy by £1.4 billion. It either assumed that longer hours would increase the temptation to buy, which is hardly ethical (Jesus condemned people who caused others to stumble[42]), or overlooked the fact that it would merely spread potential consumer spending more thinly across the week. Either way, it was mammon that was being served.

Two decades before the 2008 crash, commentator Anthony Sampson likened money and the economy to a religion that 'binds together different parts of the world, providing the means by which people and nations judge each other'. It also, he continued, 'demands great faith, [and] a huge priesthood with rituals and incantations which few ordinary people understand'.[43]

And two centuries before the crash, the 'father' of modern economics, Adam Smith, suggested that a largely benevolent 'invisible hand' was guiding the economy. He believed that self-interest, as opposed to government regulation, would lead to a balanced market as demand for goods was matched by supply. That principle soon became an article of faith equivalent to 'I believe in God Almighty' in the Christian creed. Economists who dared to challenge it were treated as pariahs, and there is still strong resistance to more than light-touch regulation of the markets.

The consensus of opinion about the cause of the crash is that, greedy and lawless traders notwithstanding, it was the *system* that failed. It was the system that kept interest rates low to stimulate spending. It was the system that encouraged a huge rise in personal and corporate debt.

The respected economist and head of the US Federal Reserve for 18 years until 2006, Alan Greenspan, had been a passionate advocate of the benevolent invisible hand model of economics. Two years after his retirement, in the aftermath of the crash, he admitted to a Senate Committee that he had made a mistake. 'To exist you need an ideology,' he said. 'The question is whether it is accurate or not … I found a flaw in the model that I perceived as the critical functioning structure that defines how the world works.'[44] His god had failed to deliver the goods, as idols always do. Greenspan had not taken into account the fact that self-interest competes with social responsibility.

St Paul wrote of fighting a spiritual war 'against the rulers, against the authorities, against the powers of this dark world and against the spiritual forces of evil in the heavenly realms'. There are also New Testament references to 'the prince of this world' and 'the god of this age', generally interpreted as the fallen angel Satan intent on diverting people from the priorities of God.[45] Such statements are sometimes taken to refer to demonic guerrillas disrupting everyday life with petty attacks. Perhaps they do.

But perhaps also Paul had glimpsed something beyond the personal battle with trouble and temptation. The 'systems' which people seem unable to control exert huge power over the lives of millions. They give the appearance of being driven by unseen forces. Human systems, institutions and markets have a momentum, if not a mind, of their own. Many are guided by algorithms; people are not allowed to use their common sense to override what the digital oracle tells them. The Matrix rules, and people suffer.

If there are spiritual opponents of God's good purposes for humankind, then the god of this world isn't only interested in tripping up hapless believers. It is intent on creating widespread chaos. But it can be resisted and defeated. As we saw in the previous chapter, it is *people* who choose to follow the desires and priorities of their own hearts, whatever pressure dark forces might exert. We are not helpless pawns even in the face of powerful financial systems. People developed them; people could modify them – if they wanted to.

Reviewing the great financial depression of the 1930s, the then President of the United States, Franklin D. Roosevelt, used his 1933 inaugural address to condemn the 'unscrupulous money changers' of the period who 'know only the rules of a generation of self-seekers. They have no vision, and where there is no vision, the people perish.'

That last sentence is a quote from the Bible.[46] More recent translations render 'perish' as something like 'cast off restraint'. When the vision is to amass wealth, everyone's gloves come off and the devil can have a field day.

'Life does not consist in an abundance of possessions,' warned Jesus.[47] The enormity of that comment sometimes eludes us. Contemporary spiritual writer Richard Foster put it much more starkly: 'For Christ, money is an idolatry we must be converted *from* in order to be converted *to* him. The rejection of the god mammon is a necessary precondition to becoming a disciple of Jesus.'[48]

'Materialism' is a better term than 'money' for mammon today, because it is often what money can buy that occupies the centre of our attention. Materialism is a world-view; it determines our priorities and directs our lifestyle choices. It offers so much, yet the offer is fraudulent. Jesus described wealth as 'deceitful'.[49] Materialism is deceitful Judas in timeless clothes. Let's find some positive ways of dealing with it.

More than enough

One of the most poignant incidents in the gospels is Jesus' encounter with an earnest seeker. He *ran* to Jesus – he was that keen – with a burning question: 'What must I do to inherit eternal life?' Jesus recited some of the commandments, which the man claimed to have kept faithfully. Mark tells us that 'Jesus looked at him and *loved* him'. That's not a general statement like 'God loves everyone'. This was Jesus recognising an individual's genuine interest and concern.

So he continued, 'One thing you lack ... Go, sell everything you have and give to the poor, and you will have treasure in heaven. Then come, follow me.' Mark reports that 'the man's face fell'. It would: he was very wealthy. And he went away crestfallen.

When he had gone, Jesus told his disciples that a camel could go through a needle's eye more easily than a rich person could enter God's kingdom. They were staggered. Was that the price for everyone? If so, who ever could be saved?[50]

Although Jesus himself seems to have lived largely as a mendicant, depending for food and shelter on the hospitality of others, he never said this was to be a model for all his followers. If he had, he couldn't have enjoyed their hospitality. He wasn't interested in how much or how little a person had; he was interested in how they viewed what they had.

Everything that exists belongs to God. He made it. Yes, we have moulded it, developed it, utilised it, often to very good effect. But we can't in any meaningful sense *own* it. We have it on trust. We lease the land; we borrow its resources. God looks to us to account for our stewardship of his property, as Jesus made clear in his parable of the talents.[51]

King David, in his last recorded prayer before his death, praised God with words that are still used today at Anglican communion services: 'Yours, Lord, is the greatness and the power and the glory and the majesty and the splendour, for everything in heaven and earth is yours.' He went on to thank God for the people's gifts that would be used by his son Solomon to build a temple in Jerusalem, and added, 'all this abundance … comes from your hand, and all of it belongs to you'.[52] Our giving is merely the interest earned on God's capital.

There is more about money and possessions than about sex in the Bible. That may seem surprising, given the church's centuries-long obsession with sex. According to the gospel records, Jesus spoke more about wealth than about prayer and heaven, too. This also may seem surprising given that many church services focus on spiritual or theological matters rather than on practical matters of day-to-day discipleship. For Jesus, morality was not restricted to the bedroom and banished from the boardroom. It was not a matter of private choice but of public conduct. His fundamental message was 'Seek first [God's] kingdom and his righteousness, and all these things will be given to you as well.' God knows that we need homes, food, clothes, and hence jobs and wages. That some people lack them is a spiritual evil as well as a social scandal. God's concern is what our heart – our inner self, our emotion as well as our mind – is set upon: 'Where your treasure is, there your heart will be also.'[53]

That is what upset the rich young man. His comfort, security, identity and status were all bound up with his possessions, and they had become a spiritual impediment. For him, God's requirements were like a spare-time activity, which he pursued energetically and faithfully. He had added them to his existing lifestyle. He was unable to make the emotional and spiritual leap to focus primarily on God's requirements and relegate *everything* else to second place. The leap *is* phenomenally difficult, but not impossible, as Jesus assured his shocked and incredulous disciples.[54]

St Paul, who as a Pharisee before his conversion was probably not short of cash, wrote of how he considered all his past gains (especially his social status) as 'garbage'. His priority now was, 'I want to know Christ – yes, to know the power of his resurrection and participation in his sufferings.'[55] He was determined not to repeat Judas' error and betray his Lord by hedging his bets. Christ was first, whatever the cost in terms of personal comfort.

Was it this joyful abandonment of acquisitiveness that gave the early church its spiritual dynamic and made such an impression on the communities it touched? Christians not only met regularly for prayer and worship. They shared their goods, sold things to help the poor, so 'there was no needy person among them' and 'the Lord added to their number daily those who were being saved'.[56]

That lifestyle is sometimes admired from a distance, but is more often rejected as impractical for today. Of course, life in the twenty-first century is vastly different to that of the first century. People are not different, however, and nor are their aspirations. The principles on which the lifestyle was based are still applicable.

Becoming content

Having enough money and possessions to live comfortably without worry is clearly a good thing. But it is a myth that they can bring happiness. They can bring the opposite. When Markus Persson, the Swedish creator of the computer game Minecraft sold his company for £1.5 billion, he bought a Beverley Hills mansion, a fleet of cars and a playboy's lifestyle. In a series of tweets he admitted to feeling isolated and unhappy. He apologised for his 'whining' to people whose more basic needs were not met.

There is even a psychological condition called 'wealth fatigue syndrome', which is said to affect some mega-rich people, who seek counselling for the guilt and anxiety generated by their disproportionate riches, whether inherited or acquired. They can, of course, afford the high fees of private shrinks.

In a scathing attack on materialism, analyst Oliver James claimed that materialists 'are more emotionally insecure, have poorer quality personal relationships ... and have lower self-esteem' than unmaterialistic people. Their 'low self-esteem derives from exaggerated ideas of what wealth and possessions can deliver'.[57] We can't buy love, although in our manic drive to impress we may try to.

That may be a sweeping generalisation, but we can't escape the fact that as relative wealth has increased, so too has the incidence of anxiety, depression and other mental illnesses. With increased wealth there has come increased pressure on our time (life has speeded up) and on our expectations (our assumed right to a given standard of living). Previous generations may have had a physically harder life, but our relative ease has brought an angst they rarely knew.

However, what we style 'happiness', even with modest resources, can easily become 'complacency'. Like the rich fool in Jesus' parable, we can settle back into comfort, plan for our retirement, eat, drink and be merry, and let the world go by. Instead of building up things for ourselves, Jesus said, we should rather focus on being rich towards God.[58]

Neither anxiety nor complacency are God's intended purpose for human life. Instead, the Bible introduces us to the concept of contentment. The early Israelites were given a graphic illustration of the idea when they were wandering in the desert after their escape from slavery in Egypt.

Hungry and rebellious, they found a white, flaky honeydew-like substance on the ground which they called 'manna'. (Some similar phenomena, mostly secretions from desert insects, are known but none fully fit the biblical descriptions.) They collected and ate it each day. If they collected a surplus, it went bad. They had to be content with their daily bread, which they soon found boring. Contentment requires patience and acceptance.[59]

Contentment was a guiding principle in the New Testament. When John the Baptist was calling people to mend their ways in preparation for the coming Messiah, some soldiers asked him for practical advice. Bearing in mind that they generally supplemented their meagre wages by extortion, they received a challenging reply: 'Don't extort money and don't accuse people falsely – be content with your pay.'[60]

When Paul warned his young colleague Timothy that 'the love of money is a root of all kinds of evil', he noted that the desire to be rich can plunge people 'into ruin and destruction'. By contrast, 'godliness with contentment is great gain', and, 'if we have food and clothing, we will be content with that'. He added the obvious comment that 'we brought nothing into the world, and we can take nothing out of it.' So what's the point of amassing stuff for its own sake?[61]

Paul also told the Philippians that he had 'learned to be content whatever the circumstances', despite the many deprivations he experienced in the service of Christ. The author of Hebrews urged readers to 'keep your lives free from the love of money and be content with what you have'.[62]

That's the ideal. But where do we draw the line? What is the 'enough' with which we are to be content? Housing, yes, but what size and where, rented or owned? Food, yes, but exotic or basic, ready meals or home cooked? Clothes, yes, but designer or high street, lasting or latest fashion? Transport, yes, but bike and bus or multi-car household, gas guzzler or hybrid?

And beyond such basics, what about the 'essentials' that our great-grandparents never dreamed of and managed quite well without? Washing machine, dishwasher, tumble dryer, fridge, freezer, smartphone, computer, TV (in several rooms) and holidays. It soon becomes clear that contentment cannot be defined by an inventory. Contentment is a state of mind.

Contentment does not crave more but is satisfied with what it already has. It does not covet what others can afford but fully utilises what it possesses. Contentment seeks to conserve rather than waste. It is modest, not flashy; it values thrift, not fashion; it considers giving more than it desires to receive. Contentment is a life focused on human values and spiritual virtues; it can deliver us from the evils of avarice and is a buttress against the risks of a moral collapse.

Contentment sees its current circumstances in the context of the wider world. Former Bishop of Winchester, John V. Taylor, pointed out that the biblical word for moderation 'is not ... a yielding meekness; it means, rather, a matching, a toning in with the whole, an awareness of how one's own small piece fits into the jigsaw puzzle'.[63]

Economists will argue that contentment is the enemy of consumerism. As consumerism is the foundation of capitalism, the world economy would flatline if everyone were to practise contentment. But we could argue that people would be happier and less stressed if they did. And what, at the end of the day, is more important? If Judas had learned contentment, he might not have taken the priests' money so readily.

Learning to let go

From contentment, generosity springs. When we are content, we can let go of what we own. When we love, we can give. When we are grateful for what we have, we can share it freely with others. The disciples' horror at Mary's 'waste' of nard is a classic example of an ungenerous, discontented penny-pinching attitude. Protective acquisitiveness can be soul-destroying, perhaps without us even noticing.

Tolkien's Gollum in *The Hobbit* and *The Lord of the Rings*, clutching and then searching for his lost 'precious', the one ring to rule them all, is a model for all who obsessively cling to their good fortune. Gollum, as readers and filmgoers will recall, was a shrivelled creature, formerly a hobbit, whose mind and soul was twisted by his lust for the ring. This is what Jesus meant when he warned against gaining the whole world yet losing one's soul.[64] He wasn't talking just about a person's eternal destiny but also about their temporal well-being.

C. S. Lewis portrayed a similar character, with a vastly different outcome. In *The Great Divorce*, he imagined a trip to the spiritual sifting area in the foothills of heaven. He saw a ghost approaching, carrying a lizard on its shoulder. Despite the ghost's entreaties the lizard kept whispering in his ear. An angel offered to silence it but warned that he would have to kill it first. The ghost feared that such drastic action would kill him too. There was a tussle of wills. Eventually, the ghost gave in. The angel threw the lizard to the ground and the ghost reeled back, screaming.

And then, as the observer watched, the ghost grew into a handsome man. The lizard writhed and then slowly transformed into a magnificent stallion. The pair were reunited, and galloped off 'into the rose-brightness of that everlasting morning'.[65]

We're more authentically human without the burdens that nag us. Letting go of them can be soul-enhancing. When we learn to sit loose to what we have, when we mentally and emotionally refuse to be possessed by our belongings and bank balances, they can be transformed. We can achieve far more with them than by merely grasping them close to ourselves.

'Give,' said Jesus, 'and it will be given to you. A good measure, pressed down, shaken together and running over, will be poured into your lap. For with the measure you use, it will be measured to you.'[66] Generosity brings its own rewards. It can bring joy to the giver. It can release resources to individuals and agencies that need them more than we do.

It also promises future spiritual riches. 'Sell your possessions and give to the poor,' Jesus said. 'Provide purses

153

for yourselves that will not wear out, a treasure in heaven that will never fail'. The sentiment is repeated several times in the New Testament.[67]

There is no suggestion here that acts of charity clock up points on our heavenly credit rating to qualify us for a bigger payout when we die. Rather, giving has two spiritual effects. One, it draws us closer to the heart of God: we are doing what he wants us to do in the world, and it forces us to trust him more than our own resources. It is a practical exercise of faith that strengthens our spirit. Two, it spreads the 'aroma of the knowledge of him everywhere … the pleasing aroma of Christ … an aroma that brings life', as Paul put it, within the wider world.[68] We are creating the environment in which people may be drawn towards acknowledging God for themselves and for which they will be thankful, to God and to us, in eternity.

We are not expected to give what we cannot, only what we can; and even then, not out of duty but from compassion, because 'God loves a cheerful giver'.[69] Generosity is an expression of love and care. We may be able to help maintain church ministry and support cash-strapped charities trying to catch the people who fall through the cracks of a creaking welfare system. There may be family members, friends or neighbours we could sponsor or support, so they can gain qualifications, start a business, get back on their feet, or just survive a difficult time.

Richard Foster bluntly states that 'the proper use of money is not for living high down here; that would be a very poor investment indeed. No, the proper use of money is investing as much of it as possible in the lives of people, so that we will have treasure in heaven'.[70]

We noted earlier how charitable giving tends to decrease proportionally as people's incomes grow, so it is important to acknowledge that there are exceptions. TV journalist Robert Peston tells of Chris Hohn, a hedge fund manager whose company gives to charity 0.5 per cent of its assets and an additional five per cent if the return on its funds exceeds ten per cent. Not all hedge funds are greedy.[71]

A handful of multi-millionaires, among them the American investor Warren Buffett and Microsoft founder Bill Gates, have pledged to give away most of their personal fortunes, and have set up 'The Giving Pledge' to encourage others to do the same. 'It is amazing to me,' said Buffett, 'the degree of inequality that exists without people really getting upset.'[72] This leads to the third principle of handling wealth, the one that Judas *said* most concerned him.

Addressing inequality

In his teaching about giving, Paul commended the extreme generosity of Macedonian Christians despite their 'very severe trial' (persecution) and 'extreme poverty'. He used their example to encourage the better-off Corinthian churches to do the same as a demonstration of their love for Christ. His concern, he said, was 'that there may be equality. At the present time your plenty will supply what they need, so that in turn their plenty will supply what you need.'[73]

The now discredited economic theory of a steadily growing system assumed that wealth would trickle down through society. As people at the top grew richer and companies prospered, so people lower down the social scale would benefit. Commentator and former Conservative MP Matthew Parris suggests that to ignore the growing gulf between rich and poor because overall prosperity has increased 'takes an impoverished view of the human moral imagination'. He claims that the average chief executive of one of the top 100 UK companies earns 183 times the average income of their employees; higher earning CEOs take home 810 times the income of their average employees.[74]

Nowhere does the Bible suggest that inequality will be completely eradicated, but it does expect those who are better off to alleviate poverty. 'There will always be poor people in the land', the ancient law declared. 'Therefore I command you to be open-handed towards your fellow Israelites who are poor and needy in your land.'[75]

Rather caustically, perhaps, the French theologian and sociologist Jacques Ellul once rebutted critics who considered any comment by the church about the world of economics to be misguided: 'The Bible did not have to wait for either the capitalist constitution or Marx's teachings to give us the most complete and powerful teaching regarding the poor that has ever existed.'[76]

The Bible's concern is humanitarian with a spiritual edge. People who ignored or took advantage of the poor were warned by prophets of God's judgement. True worship was seen as sharing food with the hungry and giving shelter to the poor, a view reinforced by Jesus.[77] That can only happen when we discover contentment and demonstrate generosity.

Today's problem of relative poverty (there are said to be more than 13 million people in the UK in low-income households, to say nothing of the massive inequalities elsewhere in the world) also has to be addressed corporately. For that, we have ballot boxes. Politicians, though, tend to shelter behind the wall of affordability rather than face the mountain of responsibility. To channel much-needed aid through higher taxes is political anathema. We're back to Judas: self-interest rules.

While a few people may be lazy or bring poverty on themselves and then expect others to help them, in most cases their plight is undeserved. It is hugely frightening to be dependent on an unfeeling benefits system while you are trying to find work. It is deeply embarrassing to have your bank card rejected at the till, forcing you to phone a relative for money or put back on the shelf items you really need.

Poverty isn't just demeaning; it is also depressing. And depression saps a person's energy, making it harder than ever to take the initiatives that might lead them back to dignity and self-sufficiency. Poor people need support, not just sympathy; they may need mentoring as much as money. They need to be given a break, before their plight breaks them and they join the company of the despairing and suicidal.

For among that company, long ago, was the tragic figure of Judas Iscariot. We turn from the glitter of gold to the darkness of failure, guilt and shame as Judas flees from the scene of Jesus' death towards his own self-inflicted doom.

Notes

[1] Said by a Russian woman to Ross Kemp, *Gangs*, Penguin Books, 2008, p.235.

[2] John Cassidy, *Why Markets Fail*, Penguin Books, 2010, p.168.

[3] Matthew 26:15; Luke 22:4-6.

[4] John 12:6; 13:29.

[5] Exodus 21:32; Zechariah 11:12-13.

[6] Exodus 21:2-11; Deuteronomy 15:12-18. See Amos 2:6 for condemnation of enslavement for trivial matters.

[7] Exodus 23:12.

[8] 1 Corinthians 6:19-20; Romans 6:15-23.

[9] Matthew 20:28.

[10] 1 Timothy 1:9-11. There are oblique references to the evils of slave trading in Ezekiel 27:13 and Revelation 18:13.

[11] Ephesians 6:5-9; Philemon; cf. Galatians 3:28.

[12] Information about modern slavery is freely available on the internet; useful sites include www.crimestoppers-uk.org; www.stopthetraffik.org and www.walkfree.org.

[13] Luke 4:18 quoting Isaiah 61:1-2.

[14] Quoted by John Marks, *The Search for the Manchurian Candidate*, Allen Lane, 1979, p.42.

[15] Norman Moss, *Klaus Fuchs*, Grafton Books, 1987, p.105.

[16] Deuteronomy 25:13-16; Amos 8:5-6; cf. Leviticus 19:35-36; Hosea 12:7.

[17] Deuteronomy 16:19-20.

[18] 1 Corinthians 10:12.

[19] 1 John 1:5-7.

[20] Romans 13:8-10.

[21] Acts 8:18-24.

[22] Luke 19:45-47; John 2:12-22. Jesus also exhibited verbal anger at the petty legalism of the Pharisees, Matthew 23:16-22.

[23] *The Times*, 16th June 2012.

[24] Luke 19:1-10; cf. Exodus 22:1-15; 2 Samuel 12:6.

[25] Ephesians 4:28.

[26] Luke 16:1-15.

[27] Ecclesiastes 5:10.

[28] *The Times Magazine*, 5th March 2011.

[29] Douglas Adams, *The Salmon of Doubt*, Macmillan, 2002, prologue p.xxv.

[30] *The Times*, 23rd August 2014.

[31] Anthony Sampson, *The Midas Touch*, BBC Books / Hodder & Stoughton, 1989, p.154.

[32] Jordan Belfort, *The Wolf of Wall Street*, Hodder & Stoughton, 2008, pp.33, 48. This lurid account of sex, alcohol and drug-fuelled excess was turned into a 2013 film directed by Martin Scorsese.

[33] Matthew 12:1; Mark 11:12-14, 20-22. See Leviticus 19:9-10 and Deuteronomy 23:24-25 for gleaning, and its practice in the story of Ruth 2:2-18.

[34] Leviticus 25:8-55.

[35] Matthew 18:21-35.

[36] Matthew 5:25-26.

[37] Reported in *The Times*, 9th March 2013.

[38] Larry Elliott and Dan Atkins, *The Gods That Failed*, Vintage, 2009, p.4.

[39] Matthew 7:24-27.

[40] Matthew 26:6-13; John 12:1-8.

[41] Matthew 6:24; Luke 16:13.

[42] Matthew 5:19; 18:6-9.

[43] Anthony Sampson, *op. cit.*, p.1.

[44] Quoted by John Cassidy, *How Markets Fail*, Penguin Books, 2009, p.6.

[45] Ephesians 6:12; John 12:31; 2 Corinthians 4:4.

[46] Proverbs 29:18 (King James Version).

[47] Luke 12:15.

[48] Richard Foster, *Money, Sex and Power*, Hodder & Stoughton, 1987, p.28.

[49] Mark 4:19.

[50] Mark 10:17-31.

[51] Matthew 25:14-30.

[52] 1 Chronicles 29:10-20.

[53] Matthew 6:33, 21.

[54] Mark 10:27.

[55] Philippians 3:7-11.

[56] Acts 2:42-47; 4:32-35.

[57] Oliver James, *The Selfish Capitalist*, Vermillion, 2008, pp.7, 73.

[58] Luke 12:13-21.

[59] Exodus 16:13-35; Numbers 11:4-9.

[60] Luke 3:14.

[61] 1 Timothy 6:6-10.

[62] Philippians 4:11-12; Hebrews 13:5. Paul's list of sufferings is in 2 Corinthians 11:22-33.

[63] John V. Taylor, *Enough is Enough*, SCM Press, 1975, pp.45f.

[64] Luke 9:23-25.

[65] C. S. Lewis, *The Great Divorce*, Collins, 1972, pp.89-94.

[66] Luke 6:38.

[67] Luke 12:33. See also Matthew 6:19-20; Luke 14:13-14; Galatians 6:9-10; 1 Timothy 6:18-19.

[68] 2 Corinthians 2:14-16.

[69] 2 Corinthians 9:6-11.

[70] Richard Foster, *op. cit.*, p.55.

[71] Robert Peston, *Who Runs Britain?* Hodder & Stoughton, 2008, p.211f.

[72] Quoted in *The Economist*, 19th May 2012.

[73] 2 Corinthians 8:1-15.

[74] Matthew Parris, *The Times*, 23rd January 2016.

[75] Deuteronomy 15:11.

[76] Jacques Ellul, *Money and Power*, Marshall Pickering, 1986, pp.141f.

[77] Isaiah 58:1-12; Amos 2:7, 5:11; Matthew 25:31-46.

Chapter 6
Through the valley of the shadows

Guilt and regret, doubt and despair are common experiences, and can open up a dark mental and spiritual tunnel which seems to have no end. But there can be glimmers of hope and renewal within it. We look at how we might find them and thus guide ourselves and people we're close to through the shadows.

Despair is the price one pays for setting oneself an impossible aim.[1]

It was the day before an interview for a job as a clerk in the House of Lords. William, a committed Christian, made three unsuccessful attempts to commit suicide. For weeks afterwards he suffered searing pangs of guilt, believing that he had now incurred God's judgement. Then he had a total breakdown in which he heard voices and saw hallucinations. For a while he was cared for by a compassionate church minister. Six months later the cloud lifted suddenly and he veered from misery to mania. It was typical of bipolar disorder.

In the years that followed, William suffered repeated psychotic episodes. They included hallucinations that his food was poisoned, and he heard voices that he believed were

God telling him to sacrifice himself. Multiple attempts at self-harm were thwarted by concerned friends.

He stopped going to church and was plagued with doubt and the fear of God's judgement, although he never fully lost his faith. The final half-dozen years of his life were spent in the ever-darkening gloom of paralysing depression.

This was William Cowper, the eighteenth-century poet whose well-known hymn, 'God moves in a mysterious way', was written the day before another suicide attempt. In a moment of lucidity, he wrote, 'I did not lose my senses but I lost the power to exercise them.' Another hymn, 'O for a closer walk with God', laments 'an aching void the world can never fill'. Many people who suffer from mental illness and depression could identify with those sentiments.

His life hadn't been helped by a series of traumas. His mother died when he was six. He was sent to a boarding school where he was bullied. He was prevented from marrying the love of his life, and a later soulmate died, leaving him bereft. Cowper lived long before the development of the talking therapies and drug treatments that we now use to ameliorate such symptoms. He was lucky not to have been locked up in what were then called 'lunatic asylums'.[2]

Mental illness has always plagued the human race, and in the twenty-first century it is not far from becoming an epidemic. It is reckoned that one on every four people will suffer from it at some point in their life. The World Health Organization suggests that someone in the world dies at their own hand every 40 seconds. Suicide is the biggest single cause of death for men aged 20–49. At the time of writing, there is public concern about an alarming rise in mental health issues among schoolchildren, often triggered by sexting.

You don't have to be a bad person to suffer despair and mental turmoil. It should never have been stigmatised by stiff upper lip Victorians (and their modern successors), or by Christians for whom mental illness is a sign of weak faith. Doubt, depression and despair appear regularly in the Bible and were vividly described in one of the world's best-known books.

Written in 1678, John Bunyan's *Pilgrim's Progress* shows the eponymous Pilgrim starting a journey with a burden of guilt and anxiety. He soon sank into the Slough of Despond, a swamp of doubt and fear. Having been helped out, he joyfully abandoned his burden at the cross. Then he faced numerous snares and endured an epic battle in the Valley of Humiliation. From there he entered the Valley of the Shadow of Death, inching along a precipice where he was buffeted by high winds and haunted by fiends. Passing the gaping mouth of Hell he negotiated traps and deep pits. Once through the valley he had to climb the Hill of Difficulty and resist the tempting diversions of Vanity Fair. Then he chose the easier-looking path towards the Celestial City, only to be captured by Giant Despair and locked in Doubting Castle. There, he and his companion were urged to kill themselves before the giant did it for them. At the last moment Pilgrim found the Key of Promise and the pair escaped, eventually arriving at their celestial destination.

There had been some good times along the way, too, but the point of the book was to show that life is never easy, even for someone with faith. (Bunyan wrote it in prison.) It's only the lies peddled by the snake-oil shamans of consumerism that persuade us that life should always be rosy. God is present in the valley of the shadows, but we still have to endure its terrors.[3]

So spare a thought for Judas Iscariot. What he did in betraying Christ was wrong. But he was then crippled by despair, and the violent end of his tortured life was tragic. It would be very easy to dismiss his suicide with glib judgements: 'Serves him right. He didn't deserve to live. He was an evil man. Good riddance. May he rot in hell.' Easy, but not right. There was much more to it. There always is for those who despair of life.

Falling into the swamp of despondency

Whatever Judas thought would be achieved by handing Jesus over to the authorities in a quiet night-time arrest, it was not death by crucifixion as a criminal. As soon as the sentence was passed, Matthew reports that Judas 'was seized with remorse', flung the money on the floor and said, 'I have sinned … for I have betrayed innocent blood.' He went out and hanged himself.[4] Some versions translate this as 'Judas repented', but the original word means deep regret, rather than the repentance that says sorry, seeks forgiveness and pledges itself to a new life.

Luke's account doesn't mention hanging, but that 'he fell headlong, his body burst open and all his intestines spilled out'.[5] That could, of course, be the result of a breaking rope or branch after Judas had died; scavenging birds and mammals would have immediately ripped open the body.

The accounts also differ over whether Judas bought the field before he died or if the priests bought it with Judas' discarded money. Either way, it was technically his field. Called Akeldama, the Field of Blood, it was used as a cemetery and was once a place of pilgrimage for relatives of the dead who were buried there. Today it is largely desolate, save for a small monastery dedicated to a fourth-century monk.[6]

So why did Judas commit suicide? Why does anyone? To begin to answer that, let's recall what we have seen so far of his likely personality, and in the light of that consider his possible states of mind, before looking in detail at three of the issues that are raised.

He felt hopeless and alone

Up until now, there had been no reason for the other disciples to doubt Judas. He had been one of them. He had seen Jesus raise the dead, he had heard Jesus talking about himself being raised, and above all he had heard Jesus on numerous occasions forgiving people for their sins. None of them understood the talk about resurrection, but they surely understood the concept of forgiveness.

Yet Judas was devastated. He was despairing. He was torn apart. He had messed up, big time. He was trapped, and there was no way out. It was over. All his dreams had died with Jesus. There was nothing for him to live for. Jesus was dead, and Judas was responsible. Who could he say sorry to but Jesus alone? Who apart from Jesus could forgive him? Judas had lost all hope.

Was Peter ever tempted to take the same course of action? His own betrayal of Jesus – when he denied knowing him and distanced himself from the events going on around him – evoked a similar emotion of agonising remorse: 'He went outside and wept bitterly.'[7]

Peter's tears were also for broken dreams, tinged perhaps with fear for his own life. As far as he could see, it was the end of the road for him and his friends. Regret, what might have been, hopelessness, disappointment, the devastation that only the sudden death of a much-loved friend can bring: all this must have been tearing him apart, too.

Except Peter had tried to protect Jesus in the garden. Peter wasn't responsible for the arrest. Judas was. And Judas couldn't cope with the guilt.

He was crippled by shame

Shame accompanies remorse and feelings of guilt. Shame is the emotion that makes a person want to hide from others. The humiliated person slinks away from confrontation. The hurt pride and loss of dignity can give rise to a sense of utter worthlessness, a desire to escape and to end it all.

For Judas, the sense of shame could have been made worse by the Jewish belief that hanging on a tree was seen as a sign of God's curse. Capital punishment in Old Testament times was usually by stoning or the sword. Sometimes corpses would be hung on trees as a spectacle of their disgrace. So Jesus, crucified by the Romans on a 'tree', was regarded as cursed by God, one of the images Paul used to explain the atoning effect of his death.[8]

Judas had just witnessed the man he had followed for three years humiliated and shamed. Realising his gross error of judgement, he submitted himself to that same curse, perhaps as a fitting but belated identification with his former mentor. He would have felt no hope of redemption in a future life. Nor, probably, do many people who take (or attempt to take) their own lives.

Suicide has long been regarded as deeply shameful. It was a crime on the UK statute book until 1961. Theologically it has been viewed as a major sin, usurping God's sovereign rule over a person's life and removing from them the sure and certain hope of eternal life. Suicide victims were forbidden burial in churchyards until the 1880s. Technically they were not allowed to have a formal church funeral service until very recent times, a rule which pastorally sensitive clergy overlooked.

While suicide does ignore the scriptural promises of renewal (God always offers a lifeline and a future with hope), the only 'unforgiveable sin' is the wilful attribution of an evident work of God to the devil – an extremely rare occurrence.[9] (Today's debate about assisted suicide in cases of terminal illness is more complex. It also highlights shortcomings in the provision of effective palliative and end-of-life care. It is beyond our scope here, as we consider solely the effects of personal failure.)

If shame doesn't evoke a sense of helplessness and a desire to run away, it can prompt anger, resentment and a desire for revenge. The victim may mess up, not by harming themselves but by lashing out at others. Remember that if you are ever tempted to humiliate someone. You could set off a chain reaction.

He was afraid of rejection

If Judas felt himself an outsider among the other disciples, then his remorse would have been compounded by the fact that he would have had no hope of rejoining them. All the differences that had been largely overlooked as they worked together would suddenly have resurfaced into outright hostility. He couldn't look them in the face again.

If it had been Peter who had contacted the authorities, his fellow Galileans might have sympathised with this latest of his cock-ups. But Judas? The southerner, with likely connections to the authorities? Not a chance. He was a traitor. He would be on no one's Christmas card list. 'We always knew he was different. We should have seen it coming.'

Judas couldn't face going back, apologising and explaining why he had acted that way. Besides, he'd seen Peter take a swing at the high priest's servant with a sword, and slice off his ear.[10] Presumably he still had the sword. If Judas went back, who knew if Peter, with his reputation for hot-headedness, might not use it more lethally – on him?

He was angry with himself

To his guilt, regret, isolation, shame and fear was probably added frustration. Looking back over the previous 48 hours, it should have been obvious to Judas that Jesus had been trying to give him a chance to change his mind: the sign of friendship at the last supper, the whispered conversation, the likely look of sadness and resignation in Jesus' eyes. Even Jesus' last words to him in the garden must have seared his conscience: 'Do what you came for, friend.'[11] *Friend*. Not foe.

Why hadn't he listened? Why had he been so headstrong? Why had he blundered on blindly to pursue his private agenda? Why had he given in to his determination to act alone? Why might he have assumed that the authorities, who had made no secret of their enmity towards Jesus, would now preserve him rather than punish him?

Why, above all, had he not believed that Jesus knew what he was doing? He had seen Jesus perform miracles, for goodness' sake! Jesus had walked on water, healed the sick, multiplied the loaves and fishes. Judas didn't understand all the teaching about turning the other cheek, rising from the dead, about God's fatherly love. But surely there had been enough evidence over the past three years to convince him that Jesus could be trusted?

Such eye-opening realisations when it's too late to backtrack can cause deep frustration. That creates anger with oneself, which in turn can lead to despair. Few people can walk away from such a monumental failure and carry on without feeling that a monster inside is tearing them apart. 'If only' is the cry of dereliction of a tortured soul who longs to go back and do everything differently.

He felt utterly powerless

But no one can go back. What is done is done. Now, perhaps, the folly of the deal with the priests was hammering at Judas' brain. He was powerless to stop their tide of hate sweeping Jesus away. He had sold his old friend to murderers who cared nothing for Jesus' innocence and only about his inconvenient challenge to their power and authority. Jesus had dissed them, and like street gangs protecting their territory, they had to punish such disrespect brutally as an example to others.

Judas' futile gesture of flinging the money down at the priests' feet showed his annoyance at having been hoodwinked. If he had ever hated Jesus, he hated himself more now. And self-loathing is a close relative of self-harm. Jesus' message of God's love, if dimly recalled at all, would now be falling on deaf ears. In his intense bitterness, Judas could never imagine anyone loving him.

He needed that kindly cleric who centuries later cared for William Cowper, but there was no such comforter on hand. The authorities had finished with him. The news of his mercenary betrayal would sour even the old relationships he had enjoyed before Jesus came on the scene. No one would trust Judas again.

As the unearthly gloom settled over Calvary where Jesus hung on the cross,[12] an even deeper, colder night must have pierced Judas' heart. He hastened to his end expecting, no doubt, to enter the merciless pitch darkness of oblivion.

169

Carrying the burden of guilt

Judas was guilty of a monumental error. Driven by an overpowering sense of guilt, he went on to mess up a second time by taking his own life. He assumed that there could be no forgiveness; that there was no second chance, no possibility of rebuilding his life or making amends. He was wrong.

Guilt is crippling. Like anxiety, to which it is related, it can dominate a person's mind and release hormones that may damage their health. It can contribute to a decline in mental and spiritual well-being. This was brilliantly illustrated in Fyodor Dostoevsky's nineteenth-century Russian novel *Crime and Punishment*.

The novel charts the sudden physical and gradual psychological meltdown of an impoverished student, Raskolnikov, who murdered a pawnbroker for her money. Disturbed by the old woman's sister, he murdered her too and escaped undetected, but with only a small haul of money. Although he justified his act to himself as ridding St Petersburg of a human 'vermin', his health collapsed and his behaviour became erratic. He reacted awkwardly whenever the well-reported double murder became a topic of conversation.

Following the death of a friend, he drew close to Sonya, the friend's daughter, who was a devout Christian forced into prostitution through poverty. Around the same time his path crossed that of a city investigator, Porphiry, who observed Raskolnikov's behaviour and became convinced from that alone that he was the murderer. The detective began to pressure him. Raskolnikov finally admitted his crime to Sonya, who persuaded him to confess to the authorities as his only hope of redemption. The story ends with the couple in

Siberia, where he was imprisoned, and the hint that there would be a new beginning.

Lest we believe that Raskolnikov's breakdown is merely a fictional exaggeration, consider the story of Levi Bellfield. He murdered three women, including the teenager Milly Dowler, and assaulted three others. He, too, behaved oddly after the attacks. Journalist John McShane, using previously published material, records that after the first murder Bellfield took his family for a holiday at short notice, 'a pattern he was to repeat'.

After another murder he fell into depression, and he brought forward a planned move to a new house, which was unfinished, shortly after killing Milly. Guilt, even in someone as apparently cold-blooded as Bellfield, can have strange effects.[13]

Few people need reminding that there is a lot in the Bible about sin and guilt. But there is just as much about forgiveness and redemption. The Old Testament rituals were largely concerned with the need to atone for personal and corporate sin. The death of Christ is explained partly as a sufficient and unrepeatable act of atonement for people in all generations, giving the assurance that 'if we confess our sins, he is faithful and just and will forgive us our sins and purify us from all unrighteousness'.[14]

King David arranged the battleground death of a conscientious soldier, Uriah, in order to marry his wife, Bathsheba, whom David had previously made pregnant. When his guilt was exposed, David confessed and articulated what many guilty people feel: 'I know my transgressions, and my sin is always before me.' The memory is never erased, but it doesn't have to cripple the guilty person.

David couldn't bring Uriah back, but he could pray to God for forgiveness. Wrongdoing is three-way: it harms the victim and their family, it is an offence to God who expects us to behave responsibly towards others, and it sears (or should sear) the sinner's conscience. However, David could make amends and learn from the experience. In his case that meant caring for Bathsheba and her child (who died in infancy), and promising to draw others away from wrongdoing towards serving God. So he prayed, 'Wash away all my iniquity and cleanse me from my sin.'[15]

The image of washing away guilt is very powerful (and is partly what Christian baptism in water symbolises). It reflects the 'stain' of guilt that people feel when they do wrong. Shakespeare described this in *Macbeth*. When Macbeth killed the Scottish king in order to take the throne, his wife planted the dagger on some servants. The murder spree continued in order to cover the original crimes, and Lady Macbeth frantically washes her hands and cries, 'Out damned spot!' The guilt of what had been done overpowered her.

Acknowledging rather than excusing or ignoring wrongdoing is essential for emotional and spiritual health. Some 30 years after taking part in atrocities during the dictatorship of General Pinochet in Chile, a number of former soldiers have come forward to admit their crimes. One made his confession publicly on radio in December 2015, saying he had killed at least 18 people. According to a forensic psychologist, speaking about it gave the soldiers some sort of release.[16]

A criminal who has served their sentence is no longer a criminal in the eyes of the law. They are free to start again – if the rest of the community will let them. Richard Branson, founder of the Virgin network of companies, said in an interview that he had caught employees stealing from the company but gave them a second chance. 'They've gone on to be some of the best employees we've had.' He added that the company also has a policy of taking on ex-offenders and encouraging others to do the same.[17]

It's the same in Christian theology. God *does* give us another chance; he wipes the record clean. Our sin can never come back to haunt us. At least, not from God. As far as he is concerned, forgiving is forgetting. Forgiving ourselves, though, is hard, because the feeling of guilt lingers. Yet refusing to do so is in effect calling God a liar. Counsellors sometimes encourage people suffering from guilt to be kind to themselves, rather than beat themselves up over things they cannot change. Add that to the promise that God is kind, and the advice becomes more realistic.

Being forgiven, accepting forgiveness, can be hugely liberating. Just four years before Dostoevsky published *Crime and Punishment*, the French author Victor Hugo published *Les Misérables* in 1862. It has been brought afresh to modern audiences through the stage musical and film of the same name. It has a powerful theme of forgiveness and the good that it can do (made more explicit in the film than in the book). It centres on the paroled convict Jean Valjean, who is given shelter by a bishop from whom Valjean steals the church silver. He is caught with the loot and taken back to the bishop, who explains it was given to Valjean as a gift.

Touched by the forgiveness, Valjean is transformed. He takes a new name, buys a factory and becomes mayor. When one of his workers, Fantine, is forced into prostitution and is attacked, he takes care of her and, as she dies, promises to care for her daughter. But by then he is on the run again after admitting his true identity.

During the French revolution Valjean is asked to guard a prisoner, likely to be killed. He is the policeman (Javert) who all along has been trying to arrest Valjean for breaking parole. He lets Javert go, offering the reprieve he himself has received. But Javert can't accept it, and commits suicide. It's a moving illustration of what Jesus meant in the Lord's Prayer: 'Forgive us our sins, for we also forgive everyone who sins against us.'[18]

Forgiving someone who has wronged us is never easy. Anne-Marie Cockburn's daughter died as a result of taking a 91 per cent pure Ecstasy tablet. At the end of the trial of the man who had supplied the drug, she announced her forgiveness of him. In an interview later she explained, 'It's not exactly compassion that I feel towards him. I am more interested in what he does with this. I might well be angry in the future.'[19]

Note Ms Cockburn's *attitude*: 'what he does with this'. Poet Pádraig Ó Tuama says that the Irish word for forgiveness comes from a root meaning 'good'. 'To forgive someone is "to good" them. To forgive someone is to treat them with the goodness with which they did not treat you.'[20]

Sometimes Christians feel duty-bound to forgive, but it needs to be *heart-felt* if it is to help heal the pain. Bishop Wilson of Singapore found forgiveness virtually impossible when he was tortured in a Japanese prisoner of war camp in 1943. He later explained that he coped by seeing his torturers 'not as they were, but as they had been' as children, 'and it is hard to hate little children. But even that was not enough.' He remembered a hymn which asked God to 'look on us as found in [Christ]'. That helped him to see them 'not as they had been, but as they were capable of becoming, redeemed by the power of Christ, and I knew that it was only common sense to say "forgive"'.[21]

That is what you might call 'attitude'. It is what Jesus meant when he said, 'Love your enemies, do good to those who hate you.'[22] By adopting a positive attitude – whether understanding a little of where they are coming from, feeling sorry for them, praying for them, hoping they will see the error of their ways, whatever – we are stepping out to create a more harmonious world. It is far more creative than retaliation or resentment. It is stronger than hate, because it has the power to transform lives.

Sadly, Judas didn't give the possibility of forgiveness and renewal a chance. Yet what he did next could not have been easy.

Battling the giant of despair

What went through his mind in those final minutes? Did he think of his family and old friends? Did he silently cry to God for mercy? How did he force himself to tie the knot, to resist the primal instinct of self-preservation, that powerful insistence of body and mind to fight for every last breath?

Make no mistake. Whatever you think about Judas, whatever conclusion you may reach concerning the motives behind his foolish action, suicide is never easy, for anyone. Only about one in every ten attempts is 'successful'. Maybe some are half-hearted cries for help. But any attempt is serious, a sign of deep distress. (Suicide bombers seeking to destroy others for ideological reasons are a perverted exception.)

Suicide accounts are rare in the Bible. The mortally wounded King Saul fell on his own sword to avoid the humiliation of being killed by an enemy in battle. Ahithophel, a former adviser to King David who defected to David's rebellious son Absalom, hung himself after his advice was rejected by his new employer.[23]

If suicide accounts are rare, cries of despair are not. All that Judas may have experienced – guilt and regret, shame, rejection, fear, frustration, powerlessness – can add up to the despairing feeling that life isn't worth living. The Bible is littered with examples of people who reached breaking point. People like Hagar, for example. She was Abraham's second wife who was evicted from the family home along with her son Ishmael. Hungry, thirsty and alone in the desert, she cried in desperation, 'I cannot watch the boy die.' The pair were rescued, but only at the last minute.[24]

There was no such reprieve for grieving mothers in the besieged city of Jerusalem six centuries before Christ. Jeremiah lamented, 'With their own hands compassionate women have cooked their own children, who became their food when my people were destroyed.' The children, we assume, had already died of starvation. The families would never have recovered from such trauma.[25]

Most of the biblical narrative focuses on the movers and shakers rather than ordinary citizens, of course. Many of them had a fair share of anxiety too. Moses crumbled under the pressure of work, exacerbated, no doubt, by his advanced years. 'What have I done to displease you …?' he cried to God. 'The burden is too heavy for me. If this is how you are going to treat me, please go ahead and kill me right now.'[26]

Elijah the prophet crumbled under physical exhaustion and death threats. He ran away to hide, collapsing in the desert and pleading, 'I have had enough, Lord. Take my life.'[27]

Jeremiah, sometimes called 'the weeping prophet', crumbled under constant criticism. Possessing a sensitive nature and thin skin he recoiled from his calling to announce bad news to a rebellious nation. He frequently expressed deep emotional distress. 'Cursed be the day I was born … Why did I ever come out of the womb to see trouble and sorrow and to end my days in shame?'[28]

Job, whose book explores the vexing problem of undeserved suffering, crumbled when his world fell apart and he lost everything. He, too, cursed the day he was born. 'I loathe my very life,' he admitted. 'Why did I not perish at birth?' 'My face is red with weeping ... My spirit is broken.'[29]

The various authors of the Psalms crumbled under assorted pressures, and weren't afraid of telling God what they thought of the injustice and personal agony. 'I am worn out from my groaning.' 'My heart has turned to wax; it has melted within me ... All my bones are on display.' 'You have put me in the lowest pit, in the darkest depths.' 'My heart is blighted and withered like grass; I forget to eat my food.'[30]

Even Jesus crumbled. Praying desperately in the Garden of Gethsemane for rescue from his imminent crucifixion, Jesus suffered the kind of extreme emotional distress that has powerful bodily effects. Some of his blood vessels burst under the pressure: 'His sweat was like drops of blood falling to the ground.' We think of Jesus as strong; not here. He was also 'a man of sorrows, and acquainted with grief'.[31]

Then there was Paul, the pioneer church planter. His entire post-conversion life was dogged by trouble: assassination and lynching attempts, shipwrecks, imprisonments, hunger, homelessness. So much, in fact, that he confessed to the Corinthians that 'we were under great pressure, far beyond our ability to endure, so that we despaired of life itself'.[32] He admitted to the Philippians, while he was chained to a Roman soldier, that he wondered if he could go on living. 'I desire to depart and be with Christ, which is better by far; but it is more necessary for you that I remain in the body.'[33] Somehow, he found God's strength to keep going.

These people were brutally honest but not totally hopeless. Even when they were death-desiring they were also life-affirming. They were sometimes angry with an apparently absent God, and sorry for themselves. They bemoaned their lot in life yet believed that God, somehow, was still with them in the valley of the shadows and still caring for them even though they had precious little evidence of it. Unlike Judas, they trusted that God knew what he was doing.

They believed, with Paul, that God 'will not let you be tempted beyond what you can bear'.[34] They proved it, because they bore their trials. But only by a whisker. It was never easy. Elijah discovered that he still had something to live for. Job became convinced that his redeemer lived and 'in my flesh I will see God'. The psalmist realised that the God who had acted powerfully in the past could do so again 'because of your unfailing love', mysterious as his ways were. Paul discovered that in his weakness, God was strong.[35]

It was, and still is, as Jesus had predicted: 'In this world you will have trouble. But take heart! I have overcome the world.'[36] Such promises, however, are not clichés to be dished out by the comfortable to the discomfited. Sufferers need people to sit with them and support them, as Job's friends did when they first heard of his terrible plight. Later, though, they presumed to offer analysis and advice like pundits on a sports show, and were duly reprimanded by God for their insensitivity. It was they who really messed up, not Job shouting his near-obscenities at an invisible and apparently indifferent God.[37]

The problem with despair, or any level of depression resulting from any cause, is that we cannot see a way out. Life makes an emergency stop. All that is before us is deep darkness, deafening silence, an impenetrable wall, a sheer cliff. It can lead to physical, mental and emotional sluggishness, making decision-making, initiative-taking and rational thinking next to impossible. Remember Cowper's insight: senses are not lost, but they do seize up.

All the sufferer can do is pray for help. It is a prayer that is always answered in some way, but often the answer can only be seen in retrospect, it may be different to the specific outcome requested, and is often slow in coming. We can trust that 'underneath are [God's] everlasting arms'.[38] Indeed they are, but often it's the arms of friends and family, and sometimes the kindness of strangers, that embody that divine support rather than a bolt from the blue offering a speedy solution.

Imprisoned in doubting castle

Doubt creeps up on you slowly. It lingers like a persistent winter fog, chilling the soul. Judas must have doubted something about Jesus and his mission, or he wouldn't have betrayed him. We can have doubts about anything or anyone, from the fidelity of a partner and the honesty of a colleague to the validity of faith and the truth about God. They may be less severe than despair, but no less difficult to handle.

Doubts are disorientating, leaving a person confused. Doubts can be depressing, leaving someone feeling alone or helpless. Doubts can be demoralising, reducing one's enthusiasm for church or community life. And doubts can be devastating if they lead to (or are met by) precipitate action or hurtful words.

In matters of faith, there's a fine distinction between plodding on despite having questions about things we don't understand and doubting whether our beliefs are valid. For some people, doubts can trigger disillusionment or a total loss of faith.

Valid doubts and questions (as opposed to the scornful derision offered by sceptics who have little interest in exploring faith) are very common and can be wide ranging.

Many church members are afraid to admit having them, out of fear of appearing 'unsound' or uncommitted. Some enthusiastic church members are slow to take other people's doubts seriously. They may be quick to dismiss them as the devil's mischief, and this adds to the doubter's problems.

Doubts and questions can cover a wide range of issues, such as:

- the Bible narrative, its historicity and interpretation;

- specific Christian beliefs such as the virgin birth or the resurrection of Christ;

- prayers that don't seem to have been answered;

- traumatic personal events such as sudden illness or bereavement ('God doesn't care about me');

- natural disasters or large-scale inhumanity ('How can God let this happen?');

- the inability to counter lucid and apparently rational claims made by atheists and sceptics;

- difficult ethical dilemmas such as sharp practice in business, or sexual behaviour;

- the seeming irrelevance of church worship to the daily grind and contemporary culture;

- the bad behaviour and insensitivity of other Christians;

- alternative and attractive activities or lifestyles competing for our time and attention;

- feelings of inadequacy to fulfil a 'calling' to ministry or service, or burnout from it;

- a sense of God's absence resulting from emotional or physical factors, low mood or depression.

When we listen to people who have suffered doubts or loss of faith, we soon discover that their journey wasn't easy, nor their reasons simple. Other people, usually inadvertently, can make their problem worse. Neat explanations by believers can be used to dismiss the person's experience: 'Obviously their faith was never genuine.' Whatever 'genuine' in fallible humans ever is, 'deconverted' former believers were mostly never play-acting in their previous faith life. We must give them some credit.

The veteran broadcaster Ludwig Kennedy, who died in 2009, was nurtured in a devout Christian home. Doubts emerged in his mind when he was at Eton, and don't appear to have been addressed by teachers or chaplains. At the start of the Second World War, he enlisted as a midshipman, and his father, a retired naval commander, re-enlisted. While training, Kennedy found a book of prayers, some banal, some helpful, and he knew that his father would be praying morning and night, as he always had.

His father's ship was sunk after only a few months, with the loss of all on board. It affected Kennedy deeply. From then on, prayers 'sounded depressingly hollow'. He concluded, 'God was indifferent to people's prayers, even assuming he heard them.' He drifted further from his faith and became a humanist.[39]

Douglas Adams, the author of *The Hitchhiker's Guide to the Galaxy*, was an active Christian in his teens. He described how one day he listened to a street evangelist who he felt 'was talking complete nonsense'. The standards of argument and logic applied to other disciplines were simply ignored, and what he heard was 'embarrassingly childish'. He kept reading and thinking for a while, but later became an atheist.[40]

The illusionist Derren Brown, whom we met in chapter 4 as he persuaded volunteers to 'kill' someone, was also an active teenage Christian and fervent evangelist in a Pentecostal church. As a budding illusionist he learned to manipulate people for his act, and concluded that charismatic Christianity was similarly manipulative. His act also came in for strong criticism and opposition from Christians who considered such entertainment to be demonic. He too became an atheist.

Christian commentator Martin Saunders suggests that Brown highlights important failings in the church and 'compels us to put our house in order'. Even more worryingly, he adds, 'His remarkable popularity means that many people now approach the idea of faith with new levels of cynicism.'[41]

Both Brown and Adams are pertinent reminders that unthinking ministry and insensitive and irrational criticism of others not only deeply hurts individuals, but it also contributes to their loss of faith. The victims go on to skew the circles they move in against religion. In these two cases, the audiences are large.

St Matthew quotes the prophet Isaiah to stress how Jesus, as the servant of God, handled people whose faith was fragile or tested: 'A bruised reed he will not break, and a smouldering wick he will not snuff out.'[42] Gentleness with others is a sign of strength, not weakness. Jesus warned thoughtless people that causing others to sin was woeful and deserving of punishment.[43]

Not every church member who suffers doubt and questions leaves the church, but sadly, when they do, often their former Christian friends cut them off. British Methodist Andy Frost tells the story of Bethan. She was from an atheist home and had experienced an eating disorder and rape before she became a Christian during a student placement in Japan. Then she became ill, and couldn't understand why God allowed it. Frost reports that 'she had been through a discipleship course ... yet she was not being successfully discipled. She was struggling with the concept of suffering ... and she was carrying so much baggage that at church all she could do was cry.' Largely unsupported, she gave up her faith. By leaving church she also left the Christian community – which other leavers say is sometimes the hardest thing to do. Only her Christian friend Hannah stuck with her. Hannah offered support, not censure. Once she sent Bethan a text: 'Don't stop looking for God; he'll never stop looking for you.' That is always true, and unlike some in her position, Bethan did rediscover God. But it had been a tortuous journey.[44]

Faith journeys often are. We should never give up on anyone. The journey doesn't end until they die. The novelist and biographer A. N. Wilson seems to have been right round the block. Having hovered over the landscape of faith for much of his life, in 1989 he became what he called 'a born-again atheist', experiencing a sense of liberation from what he felt was nonsense. But it didn't last. 'My doubting temperament ... made me a very unconvincing atheist.' His love of language and the arts, and his observations of human nature, 'convince me that we are spiritual beings, and that the religion of the incarnation, asserting that God made humanity in His image, and continually restores humanity in His image, is simply true.' He returned to Christianity 'as a working blueprint for life'.[45]

Sunday church attendance statistics, which for decades have shown a steady decline in the UK, are not a completely fair measure of the level of faith within the population. They do not always include small 'new' churches, which may cream people off from traditional denominations, and they may not accurately account for midweek gatherings which become 'church' for people whose work or family commitments rule out Sunday worship.

New Zealand church minister and sociologist Alan Jamieson researched people who left church but did not reject their Christian faith. Their reasons for leaving were varied, but in most cases leaving was a last resort, when they had exhausted all other possibilities. 'Leavers are far more open to discussion than church leaders might expect,' he wrote.[46]

While there are always two sides to any separation, we tend to give 'ours' less weight than 'theirs'. So we don't invest resources to give people the opportunity to discuss doubts openly, and instead assume it's their problem to find answers to their questions. It's not always the doubters who mess up and betray their former faith; the faithful can fail them, and hence betray the spirit of their own faith, too.

If we want to help people avoid falling into a cellar, it's a good idea to close the trapdoor. Or, to change the metaphor, in Jesus' parable of the sower he predicted that some people would fall away because they had shallow roots or were choked by weeds. But every gardener knows that if you want a good crop, you clear away the stones and regularly hoe the weeds. That necessary maintenance, in faith terms, is the role of the teaching and apologetics ministry and a supportive and understanding church community.[47]

The faithful, busy with their own lives, can also fail to notice the tiny seeds of spiritual interest that sprout in unexpected places. When they are expressed by public figures we can be sure that they are shared by many. The effect of not noticing, however, is that we don't provide appropriate and unthreatening opportunities to nurture them.

Newspaper editor Amol Rajan, 'a non-believer since the age of 15', attended a Christmas service at a rural church and felt a sense of transcendence. 'Despite the supposed clarity of their conviction, the irreligious often yearn for the enduring consolations of faith, knowing them to be somehow out of reach,' he wrote.[48]

Times columnist Janice Turner confessed that 'while intellectually I am on the side of Richard Dawkins, facing down the bigotry and illogic of belief … my soul has needs that science alone cannot address'.[49] Another newspaper columnist, Rebecca Armstrong, whose husband was paralysed in an accident, wrote, 'I'm not alone in having a certain ambivalence in my beliefs, or lack thereof.' She found comfort in the fact that people were praying for Nick. 'While I don't have a faith, I do have faith in others' beliefs.'[50]

Doubt can be the friend of faith, not its enemy. Doubt can help both seeker and believer to discover more, if they have a mind to. When he faced the devastating loss of his wife through cancer, the faith of writer and university professor C. S. Lewis was shaken to its core. 'My idea of God,' he reflected, 'is not a divine idea. It has to be shattered time after time.' So it does for all of us. Growth in faith involves being stretched and asking questions.[51]

Doubt can become a learning experience. Thomas refused to believe that Jesus was risen from the dead unless he could touch the nail and sword holes in his master's body. Jesus duly appeared to him and evoked worship from Thomas. In so doing, says author Philip Yancey, 'he "broke his own rules" about faith. He made his identity so obvious that no disciple could ever deny him again (and none did).'[52] A former Lord Chief Justice of England once concluded that the evidence for the resurrection was enough to convince any jury.[53]

Doubt can be an opportunity to check, revise, discuss and strengthen our beliefs, and to admit that we can *never* know all that there is to know. 'Did God really say, "You must not eat from any tree in the garden"?' was the whisper Eve heard in the garden. She could have looked at what she knew thus far, and argued back, 'No, he didn't. He only said there's one we must avoid; I don't know why, but he's been good so I'll trust that he knows best.' Then she would have been better equipped to deal with the blatant lie that followed, pitting the devil's assurance that she would not die against God's assertion that she would. She had no idea then what death was; the real issue was which voice did she trust?[54]

So when the psalmists were faced with dire circumstances that appeared to suggest that God had deserted them, they clung to what they did know: 'I will remember the deeds of the Lord; yes I will remember your miracles of long ago.' They believed that God was unchanging even when he mystified or annoyed them.[55]

The book of Ecclesiastes in the Old Testament is a book of doubt. It repeatedly concludes that everything – the highest pleasure and the lowest suffering – is meaningless. It asks, what is the point of life? There isn't one, it says – unless, that is, God is somehow in charge, beyond our comprehension, so 'remember your Creator in the days of your youth, before the days of trouble come'.[56]

Twice in the desert before he began his ministry Jesus heard the doubting voice say, '*If* you are the Son of God…', and once he faced its direct challenge to walk away from his calling. He, too, trusted what he already knew. He countered the temptations with God's own principles recorded in the ancient Scriptures.[57] Holding fast to what we do know, however little it is, is a good strategy.

The problem with faith, of course, is that there's always a seemingly plausible alternative. And that induces a massive dilemma if you are caught between a rock and a hard place.

When do you blow the whistle?

This is where Judas could have been, according to one of the scenarios we have considered. He may have wanted to expose Jesus as a fraud, or as a liberator.

People in an organisation are occasionally drawn into, or become aware of, unethical practices or cover-ups when an innocent third party has been hurt. If they work in the public sector, they may be trusted with classified information which, for various reasons, they believe should be released in the public interest. Such scenarios create a spiritual, mental and emotional tug of war that is not unlike that of the person suffering from doubt. What do they do?

Despite legislation, supposed organisational 'transparency' and hotlines making whistle-blowing theoretically easier, it is never easy. There is always pressure to toe the line. Intimidation can be subtle but scary. Even if a complaint or report is upheld, it could be impossible to continue working with former colleagues. One's job may ultimately be at stake, and that is a difficult situation to face.

So, too, was the long-running child abuse committed by the entertainer Jimmy Savile. Exposed only after his death, investigations showed two things. One was a wilful refusal to believe often vulnerable young people when they did complain. The other was the wilful refusal of people in authority to properly investigate rumours because Savile was a big earner for the BBC and had friends in high places. No one who knew his habits of entertaining youngsters alone dared speak up, and managers' meek questions were easily brushed aside.

It's not a new problem. During Stalin's reign of terror in Russia in the first half of the twentieth century, people were silenced by the regime's paranoid response to any hint of dissent. Historian Orlando Figes was told by one survivor that even into the modern era 'I am still afraid to talk. I cannot stand up for myself or speak out in public. I always give in without saying a word ... Even today, if I see a policeman, I begin to shake with fear.'[58]

Not surprisingly, there is divided opinion in the community and the church about when and how whistles should be blown. To some people, Julian Assange is a hero of free speech; the Wikileaks organisation he founded has published more than ten million classified documents hacked or leaked from secret government sources. To others, such indiscriminate acts are criminal theft and put national and personal security at risk.

Biblical principles are hard to come by. There is a place for secrecy. As we keep noticing, God has his secrets which we can never fathom. 'The secret things belong to the Lord our God, but the things revealed belong to us and to our children for ever, that we may follow all the words of [his] law.'[59] In personal relationships, observing confidentiality is a virtue not a vice: 'A gossip betrays a confidence, but a trustworthy person keeps a secret.'[60]

Criminal or immoral secrets, by contrast, will be judged by God and laid open to view, which suggests that sometimes courageous exposure of wrongdoing can be justified. In personal behaviour, Paul says, 'we have renounced secret and shameful ways; we do not use deception'.[61] Truth is desired by God and is to be spoken from the heart.[62] Jesus called himself 'the truth', and truth is to be the belt of the Christian's 'armour' against evil, holding all the other items in place.[63]

It's not a lot to build ethical principles on. If a civil servant strongly disagrees with official policy or practice, it's arguable that they should resign rather than reveal privileged information. However, if a government department is paying backhanders or is involved in illicit arms trading, then there's a case for speaking up. The question then is, to whom do you speak? As we shall see in the next chapter, 'going public' isn't always wise or ethical even though it's much easier than following established procedures.

When a colleague is apparently acting incompetently or illegally, going public is generally not an option – it's not a matter of public interest (so the media probably won't be interested) and it may open the exposer to libel or slander charges. Then, the only choice is between keeping quiet or invoking the organisation's complaints procedures.

So what do you do? You could:

- talk in confidence to people you trust and whose judgement you value, and consider their advice;

- collect information about the situation carefully and record it safely;

- consider what you don't know: why is this going on? What may be causing someone to act as they do?

- think about how you can express your concerns in a non-confrontational manner;

- consider whether you can suggest positive changes that might resolve the situation without rancour;

- follow procedures carefully so that you are not labelled as a trouble-maker;

- take your time and don't act precipitately;

- accept that life often requires compromises; you won't always get your own way or your own views accepted;

- be gracious, even if you are angry.

Ted Kaczynski won fame (or infamy), and a life sentence, as the so-called Unabomber. A Harvard student and child prodigy, he became a recluse and engaged in a US-wide bombing campaign directed against modern technology between 1978 and 1995. He was eventually arrested with help from his younger brother David, who was promised anonymity by the FBI but was exposed in a leak.

In an interview with *Time* magazine, David spoke of his own conflicts. 'I don't feel that I did *wrong*' in exposing his brother, he said. 'On the other hand, there are tremendously complicated feelings not just about the decision itself but a lifetime of a relationship in which one brother failed to help protect another.'[64] One might add that the anonymous person who leaked his identity only added to his conflicts.

The light in the valley of the shadows is dim at best, more a guttering flame than a glaring floodlight. Progress through it can be painful and slow. Travellers can emerge from it bruised and shaken. Some are never quite the same again. Never underestimate it. But it has does have a guide and an exit. 'Even though I walk through the darkest valley, I fear no evil; for you are with me; your rod and your staff – they comfort me.'[65]

But whether in the valley or not, beware: there are trolls about…

Notes

[1] Graham Greene, *The Heart of the Matter*, William Heinemann, 1948, p.60.
[2] Details of William Cowper's life are widely available and some here are drawn from Virginia Stem Owens, 'The Dark Side of Grace', *Christianity Today*, 19th July 1993.
[3] Psalm 23:4.

4 Matthew 27:3-10.

5 Acts 1:18-19.

6 Peter Stanford describes the place in some detail in *Judas*, Hodder & Stoughton, 2015, pp.1-19.

7 Matthew 26:69-75.

8 For the curse, see Deuteronomy 21:23 and Galatians 3:13; for examples of disgraced corpses, see Joshua 10:26, 2 Samuel 21:12.

9 Matthew 12:22-32. For hope in extreme situations, see Isaiah 40:28-31; Jeremiah 29:10-14; Lamentations 3:19-33; Romans 5:1-5.

10 Matthew 26:50-54.

11 Matthew 26:50.

12 Matthew 27:45.

13 John McShane, *Predator*, John Blake, 2011, p.112ff.

14 1 John 1:9; cf. John 1:29; Hebrews 1:3, 10:1-18.

15 Psalm 51; cf. 2 Samuel 11:1–12:25.

16 Reported in *i*, 31st December 2015.

17 Interview in *Third Way*, November 2013.

18 Luke 11:4.

19 Reported in *The Times*, 15th March 2014.

20 Pádraig Ó Tuama, 'Bury the Hatchet', *Third Way*, November 2013.

21 The account and quotation is from Adrian Hastings, *A History of English Christianity 1920–1985*, Collins, 1986, pp.385f. He is citing Bishop Wilson's original account in *The Listener*, 24th October 1946.

22 Luke 6:27.

23 Saul: 1 Samuel 31:4-10, cf. 2 Samuel 21:12; Ahithophel: 2 Samuel 17:23.

24 Genesis 21:8-20.

25 Lamentations 4:10; cf. Jeremiah 19:9.

26 Numbers 11:11-15.

27 1 Kings 19:1-9.

28 Jeremiah 20:14, 18.

29 Job 10:1, 3:11, 16:16, 17:1.

30 Psalm 6:6; 22:14, 17; 88:6; 102:4.

31 Luke 22:44; Isaiah 53:3 (King James Version).

32 2 Corinthians 1:8; 11:22-33 lists his sufferings.

33 Philippians 1:23-24.

34 1 Corinthians 10:13.

35 1 Kings 19:12; Job 19:25-27; Psalm 44 (verse 26); 2 Corinthians 12:9.

[36] John 16:33.

[37] The friends' silent sympathy is described in Job 2:11-13. The rest of the book is their dialogue with Job until God's final intervention in chapters 38–41. It ended happily in chapter 42.

[38] Deuteronomy 33:27.

[39] Ludwig Kennedy, 'Getting on the Wrong Side of God', *Sunday Times*, 20th December 1998; an advance extract from his book *All in the Mind*, Hodder & Stoughton, 1999.

[40] Douglas Adams in an interview in *American Atheists*, vol. 37, no. 1, reprinted in Douglas Adams, *The Salmon of Doubt*, Macmillan, 2002, pp.97-99.

[41] Martin Saunders, 'Master of Manipulation', *Christianity*, January 2012.

[42] Matthew 12:20; Isaiah 42:3.

[43] Matthew 18:6-9.

[44] Andy Frost, *Losing Faith*, Authentic Media 2010, pp.1-16.

[45] A. N. Wilson, 'My Departure From Faith was Like a Conversion on the Road to Damascus. Now I Believe Again', *New Statesman*, 6th April 2009.

[46] Alan Jamieson, *A Churchless Faith*, SPCK 2002, p.150. He also set up an umbrella organisation called Spirited Exchanges for people who want to explore questions and doubts: www.spiritedexchanges.org.nz (accessed 23rd June 2016).

[47] Luke 8:4-15.

[48] Amol Rajan, 'Religious Lessons of Christmas for a Non-believer', *i*, 27th December 2011.

[49] Janice Turner, 'God May Not be Great but Religion Can Be', *The Times*, 20th January 2012.

[50] Rebecca Armstrong, 'Belief, Even From Others, Reveals the Soul in Us All', *i*, 3rd June 2014.

[51] C. S. Lewis, *A Grief Observed*, Faber & Faber, 1968, p.52.

[52] John 20:24-29; Philip Yancey, *The Jesus I Never Knew*, Marshall Pickering, 2000, p.214.

[53] Cited by Michael Green, *Man Alive!* InterVarsity Press, 1972, pp.53-54.

[54] Genesis 3:1-13.

[55] Psalm 77 (verse 11); cf. Malachi 3:6; Hebrews 13:8.

[56] Ecclesiastes 12:1.

[57] Luke 4:1-13, italics mine.

[58] Orlando Figes, *The Whisperers*, Penguin Books, 2008, p.252.

[59] Deuteronomy 29:29.

[60] Proverbs 11:13.

[61] Romans 2:16; 2 Corinthians 4:2.

[62] Psalm 51:6; 15:2.

[63] John 14:6; Ephesians 6:14.

[64] *Time*, 18th October 1999.

[65] Psalm 23:4 (New Revised Standard Version).

Chapter 7
Step off the rumour mill

The world is awash with rumours, allegations, innuendoes, angry verbal attacks, carping criticism and plain lies. It always has been, but today they spread more quickly than ever. They distort truth and hinder community cohesion and personal relationships. They have even twisted the facts about Judas. They are remarkably easy to start and horrendously difficult to stop. Addressing them (and their root causes) is a priority for anyone who doesn't want to poison their own mind, and who wants to make the world a better place.

> *Often evil is believed and spoken more readily about another than good. But mature people do not easily believe every teller of tales, because they know that human weakness is prone to evil and unreliable enough in speech. (Thomas à Kempis)[1]*

So far we have seen how easy it is to mess up in both small and large ways. Through it we have noticed, faintly at times, perhaps, that part of the remedy is to change the way we think about others and to challenge our own established attitudes. Now, as we draw towards the climax, we need to get a bit more personal, more honest. We're going to look deeper inside at common attitudes and assumptions that can be flawed and harmful but which are rarely questioned. But first, let's listen to Malala.

Malala Yousafzai was 15 when Taliban gunmen boarded her school bus, singled her out and shot her in the head. Remarkably, she survived, and in 2014 became the youngest-ever recipient of the Nobel Peace Prize for her work promoting girls' education in her native Pakistan and around the world.

In the story of her young life, Malala confesses that 'our people see conspiracies behind everything'. She highlights several: that the Israelis destroyed the World Trade Center to provoke America into a war on the Muslim world; that polio vaccinations were an American plot to infect women so that the Muslims in the Swat Valley (her homeland) would die out; that her own father had shot her so that the family could move to the West.[2]

'Her people' are not alone in subscribing to all kinds of way-out theories and rumours. Americans and Europeans believe that crashed alien spacecraft are stored in Area 51, an Air Force base south of Las Vegas, and that the American government is in contact with extra-terrestrial beings. Surveys have consistently shown that more than 50 per cent of Republican voters in the US believe that President Barak Obama (their political opponent) is a Muslim and was born in Africa, neither of which is true – look at the evidence.

Worse still is the opinion of a Ku Klux Klan official who said on camera for a TV documentary that God made humans white but some became black when they mated with apes. How can someone fly in the face of basic science that skin colour was originally determined by the melanin required to deal with UV rays from the sun at different latitudes? But they do. And to them, they are not 'extreme'.

The harsh fact is that we believe what we want to believe. We accept ideas or views that make us feel comfortable and confirm us in our chosen lifestyle, beliefs and outlook. Counter-evidence can even have the effect of confirming our beliefs; to change our minds presents a major threat to our sense of identity. Yet false views about people can be destructive – to ourselves, as well as to them.

'I'm amazed at how often the immediate cause of a conflict is a mistake, unfounded suspicion or rumour,' wrote Malcolm White in a magisterial survey of violence throughout history. 'History would be a lot more pleasant if people didn't rush into things.'[3]

Indeed. So back to Judas Iscariot. Because he betrayed Jesus Christ, he has been vilified and lampooned down the centuries on spurious grounds. Worse still, he has been used as an excuse for hateful attitudes and evil actions, including what is arguably the worst atrocity in history. Millions have been punished for what this one tragic individual did. He provides a classic example of how rumours, exaggerations and pure hate can distort truth and create widespread misery.

Judas betrayed

There is no contemporary record of what Judas looked like. Nor is there any contemporary record of what Jesus Christ looked like. We think we know, because artists since the Middle Ages have portrayed him and the apostles in a certain way. Most pictures show Jesus as an unearthly angelic being, a medieval prince or, more recently, a tall, light-skinned, fair-haired and blue-eyed Hollywood star. Judas, by contrast, is often portrayed as a shifty, usually darker, smaller figure.

However, Jesus and Judas (and all the other apostles) were Near Eastern Jews living in the first century AD. They would have been shorter than the average person today. They were darker skinned than most Europeans in any century – probably olive-skinned (white supremacists take note).

Later, the first Christians met in Jewish synagogues. They were regarded by the Roman authorities as a Jewish sect, which protected them from state persecution. They even debated whether non-Jews could be true Christians if they didn't also observe certain Jewish ceremonies. The argument was won by Paul and others who asserted, 'There is no longer Jew or Greek, there is no longer slave or free, there is no longer male or female; for all of you are one in Christ Jesus.'[4] God does not discriminate; therefore, the New Testament asserts, neither should we.

Yet in a survey in the United States, 'five times as many Protestants identify Peter, Paul, and other disciples as Christians rather than as Jews. When it comes to Judas, however, nearly twice as many identify him as a Jew rather than a Christian!'[5]

Stereotypes have a long shelf life. From earliest times Judas was used by writers and artists to suggest that 'therefore' all Jewish people were unreliable, traitorous and mercenary. Jerome, the fourth-century translator of the Bible into Latin, wrote, 'In Judas the Jews may be accursed ... Who do you suppose are the sons of Judas? The Jews.' A fifth-century pope, Gelasius, said that 'as Judas was called a devil and the devil's workman he gives his name to the whole race'.[6]

Papias, Bishop of Hierapolis in the early second century, elaborated on Judas' supposed physical appearance. He suggested that Judas' 'genitals were repellent and huge beyond all shamelessness', and that Judas survived his suicide attempt and became grotesquely obese.[7] This gave birth to a legend. From about the thirteenth century onwards, Christian art began showing Judas as physically hideous.

From that, it was only a small step to portraying all Jews in a similar manner. Historian Hyam Maccoby concludes, 'One cannot help seeing [in Papias' exaggerations] a forerunner of the priapic [permanently erect] Jew, who in medieval and Nazi propaganda, threatened the pure virgins of Christendom or the Aryan race with his enormous and repulsive appetites.'[8]

The habit of blaming 'the Jews' as a whole for the trial and crucifixion of Jesus added to the growth of anti-Semitism. In fact, it was only a small group of jealous religious and political leaders who engineered his death. It was the Romans (Italians in our terms) who carried out the execution, and could have stopped it had the local governor Pontius Pilate been stronger-willed. But no one has ever blamed the Italians, perhaps because Rome became a major centre of Christianity.

Discussing Adolf Hitler's genocide of some six million Jews during the Second World War, one writer suggests that 'Judasness is seen as central to the vision of Jewishness in Hitler's rhetoric'.[9] The Roman Catholic Church only officially dropped the charge of deicide – killing God – against 'the Jews' in 1965. Apologies by popes and archbishops, particularly for the Second World War Holocaust, came even later, but cannot undo the evils done to Jewish families over the past two millennia, sometimes in the name of Christ.

Do you see what damage wild assertions can do? James in the New Testament suggests that we 'consider what a great forest is set on fire by a small spark. The tongue also is a fire...'[10] Sweeping generalisations save us the bother of treating individuals on their own merits – even though we would hope they would treat us on our merits. Generalisations enable us to buy into a prevailing attitude without having to think it through for ourselves. Thus are great masses of people swayed by eloquent rhetoric and easy sound bites.[11]

The final insult – assumed unthinkingly by almost everyone – has been the confident consignment of Judas to rot in hell forever. Maybe he does, but we have absolutely no way of knowing the final destiny of him or anyone else. Jesus, who spoke a good deal about hell, forbade speculation about anything to do with the future. The New Testament message is simply to sort yourself out and leave decisions about others to God.[12] They're God's problem, not ours.

Jesus did once describe Judas as 'the son of perdition'. It means one who is lost – and he certainly was lost to the original band of 12 apostles, which is the immediate context of the statement. As the term is also applied (once) to the devil by St Paul,[13] it is logical to suggest that it might also refer to eternal banishment from God's presence. However, the possible reasons for Judas' suicide, which we explored in the previous chapter, make speculation about his destiny even more futile.

And that's as far as we can go. We don't know what goes on between a person and God in the final moments of this life as they pass towards the next. Had we been standing at the foot of the cross, we might have taken issue with Jesus' last-minute reprieve of the criminal hanging next to him ('Today you will be with me in paradise'[14]), especially if he had stolen our property or assaulted our friend and not even said sorry to his victims. We can't know, so we shouldn't guess. (Nor should we get too hung up on the imagery of burning, either; it may mean something different to the literal everlasting bonfire.[15])

However, despite the caveats, Judas has been subject to some lurid speculation about his eternal state. One tradition leaves him rattling around in hell with only King Herod (who attempted to kill the infant Jesus by ordering the slaughter of babies in Bethlehem) and Cain (who committed the first murder recorded in the Bible) for company. All other notorious Bible characters were (allegedly) given a royal pardon. This is the result of a dubious tradition called 'the harrowing of hell'.[16]

Among the reprieved, therefore, according to this tradition, would have been Manasseh. He was an evil king of Judah who corrupted the nation's religious life and practised child sacrifice. It seems that killing kids to appease non-existent gods (idols) was considered a lesser crime than Judas' betrayal.[17] And it ignores the fact that, as we noticed in chapter 2, Cain, although punished by God, was also protected by him. Zealous, speculative theologians can be very short-sighted.

In the early fourteenth century, Dante's *Divine Comedy* portrayed hell as a series of concentric circles. Judas was stranded at the lowest level, in the ninth circle, not far from the doomed devil himself. He had Brutus and Cassius, the murderers of Caesar, for company. The three prisoners are not burning but encased forever in ice. Dante's motive for writing was more to do with the politics of his day than it was to instruct the faithful in theology, but the invention fuelled the lingering myths.[18]

An interesting off-shoot of the idea of Judas burning in hell is the habit of burning Judas as an effigy. Across Catholic Europe and South America, Easter has been marked not with the chocolate eggs of Britain, Australasia and the USA but with street parades and the burning of Judas effigies. It's still especially strong in parts of Mexico.

Life-size papier-maché models, some with masks depicting not only Judas but also hated political or other present-day figures, are strung on lines across streets and blown up with fire crackers or burned on fires on Easter Sunday. The practice was probably imported by priests who, attempting to convert native Mexicans to Christianity, wanted to suggest that Judas' treachery was defeated by the resurrection of Christ. The practice also took place in the Dingle and Toxteth districts of Liverpool up until the 1950s, for reasons no one understands (unless it was simply a Merseyside money-making enterprise!). Judas effigies were burned in the street and children would beg for money for the guy just as they also did for Guy Fawkes night in November. But it never caught on elsewhere in the city or the UK.

Today such festivals are an excuse for a party. They commemorate the victory of good over bad, and there's good reason why we should remember such events. But burning effigies (especially when effigies of living figures are substituted for historical ones) is an expression of hatred.

And hatred has two negative effects on us. First, by regarding someone as a piece of trash to be incinerated in hell (or frozen out of polite company in heaven), we cease to take them seriously. We stop regarding them as human beings who do or did things we find hard to explain but which make (or made) sense to them at the time. It excuses us from making the effort to understand their actions and learn from their mistakes. We're betraying their humanity. Not even Judas deserves that.

Second, it conveniently places us on the moral high ground from which we can look down on them with contempt without examining the uncomfortable shortcomings of our own lives. It feeds our pride. Comparisons of wrongs ('mine are less bad than yours') are of no value when the ultimate standard is God's perfection. Any wrong is a blot on the landscape, a smudge on the page. Anything less than 100 per cent in the examination of human goodness is a failure; there are no lower pass grades. The Christian message is that precisely because of our shortcomings, Christ's death and resurrection was required to atone for all.[19]

All this is an example of how we can dehumanise people, and that we do ourselves a disservice in the process. Let's move into modern era to notice some related examples and learn their lessons.

Faceless nobodies

In one episode of the TV sci-fi series *Dr Who*, the Time Lord and his companions encountered humanoid creatures with no faces. Their personalities had been leached out. Anonymity gives someone a sense of power and invincibility. He or she can say and do what they like without any personal repercussions. It's much harder to say things, or to cause physical harm, to people you are facing in real time, or who can find out where you live.

British TV actor Ross Kemp has investigated rival gangs around the world. He discovered in El Salvador that 'neither gang acknowledges the other by name – it's always "people in the other neighbourhood" or the "foreigners". Naming them would only be giving them respect.'[20]

Psychologists call this 'de-individuation'. It's regarding people as objects without individual identity. It can be a convenient defence mechanism which we employ to lessen a sense of guilt or responsibility for harm which we may cause to others. So a drone pilot aiming at buildings thousands of miles away simply sees an inanimate target, not a room full of fragile human beings. Any unfortunate non-combatant people inside or nearby are 'collateral damage'. Their families might have another view.

The men of Reserve Police Battalion 101 were mentioned in chapter 1. They were German conscripts stationed in Poland during the Second World War. They used a form of de-individuation to lessen the personal impact of their work, which was to transport Jews across the country to the gas chambers and shoot the old and weak in cold blood.

They knew the fate that awaited the people they crammed into cattle trucks. But in later war crimes trials they rarely expressed any sense of responsibility for their actions. 'Their sense of detachment from the fate of the Jews they deported was unshakable.'[21] They refused to see their cargo as individuals, simply as a faceless crowd whose destination was no concern of theirs.

Often in everyday life we just don't notice people *as people*. What was the name of the checkout assistant in your latest visit to the supermarket? (They were likely wearing a badge.) Male or female? Younger or older? Hair colour? Can you remember anything at all about them? Probably very little. They were just a blur of sweeping hands. They might just as well have been a faceless, depersonalised creature straight out of the *Dr Who* studio.

But they weren't. Like you they have a name, address, tax reference, and (probably) family and friends. Like you they eat when hungry, bleed when cut, cry when sad, laugh when happy, and do things in their spare time like play computer games or participate in extreme sports. We just took them for granted. They probably took us for granted, too.

Some of the worst offences of de-individuation can occur in the realms of public and customer service. Faceless voices in a call centre, or a government or company office, brush us off with lame excuses or point-blank refusals of help. The adviser has all the power. The caller feels helpless. Nobody seems to care. When something has gone seriously wrong it can be very hard for the people affected to uncover the truth they need to help them understand; professionals close ranks, companies refuse to accept responsibility, fearful, perhaps, of expensive litigation.

The result is twofold. First, it makes the victim angry, resentful, and liable to be similarly snappy and inconsiderate towards the next person they meet. A chain reaction has been sparked, and it rumbles on and on. Second, it extends the period of the victim's suffering, making it harder for them to come to terms with what has happened and to move on.

The person or official who is handling the complaint or the issue could do worse than have a sign on their desk: love my neighbour as much as I love myself. Justice, mercy and humility are God's basic standards for human relations; by not adhering to them we are hindering rather than helping the building of God's kingdom, which is the theological term for a better world. Sometimes, we can cement a brick in one place by some godly activity while knocking one out somewhere else by our godless attitude.

Bringing out the beast

Treating people as faceless objects is not good. Treating them as animals is even worse. In the Stanford Prison Experiment (also mentioned in chapter 1), volunteers were randomly divided into 'prisoners' and 'guards' in a sociological experiment, using carefully selected normal and stable students who were then left to themselves. The experiment degenerated into a litany of abuse and had to be halted prematurely. 'I was surprised at myself,' Guard Varnish admitted afterwards. 'I practically considered the prisoners "cattle".'[22]

In another psychosocial experiment, hospital staff swapped roles and became 'patients'. A nurse – a trained carer – who took part admitted, 'I used to look at the patients as if they were a bunch of animals; I never knew what they were going through before.'[23]

But these are just revealing insights from controlled simulations. Hopefully the people involved learned important lessons and modified their subsequent behaviour. It's a different matter outside the laboratory, where people have access to live ammunition or power over hapless prisoners. Some 500 Vietnamese villagers of all ages were killed in the My Lai massacre in 1968, when US soldiers went berserk after some of their comrades had been killed in jungle warfare by the Vietcong. 'Most people in our company didn't consider the Vietnamese human,' Lt Gen. Dennis Bunning told the Peers Inquiry in 1969.[24]

It was the same in Rwanda, where in 1994 the Hutus systematically slaughtered their former Tutsi neighbours. They regarded them as 'cockroaches' to be exterminated. 'We no longer saw a human being when we turned up a Tutsi in the swamps,' one of the militia told journalist Jean Hatzfeld. 'I mean, a person like us, sharing similar thoughts and feelings.'[25]

That's also how Stalin's activists viewed the 'kulaks', the middle class former property owners targeted by the communist regime in the 1930s. One activist recalled, 'We were trained to see the kulaks, not as human beings, but as vermin, lice, which had to be destroyed.'[26]

In the early years of the twenty-first century, Ken Davis, a night shift American military policeman working as a guard in Iraq's notorious Abu Ghraib prison, told a TV documentary, 'The higher-ups said, "Use your imagination. Break them." … It was told to all of us, they're nothing but dogs. So you start breeding that picture to people, and you start doing things to 'em that you would never dream of. And that's when it got scary.'[27]

It is significant that professional soldiers, torturers and terrorists often have to regard their victims as subhuman in order to commit atrocities while at the same time continuing with their 'normal' life. It says much about the inherent, unconscious regard that most of us have for the dignity and sanctity of human life, and how hard it is to override it. Reducing people to the status of animals makes it easier to humiliate, denigrate, mistreat and even kill them.

The US and UK military say they now train soldiers to view the enemy in their sights as a threat to life, not as an animal to be picked off like a rabbit. Personnel are also taught that prisoners are to be treated humanely and with dignity; torture is expressly forbidden. Whether that official attitude filters down to the ranks in faraway places under the stress of combat is for future historians to chronicle.

But notice this. Most people accept the need to have slaughterhouses for meat production where the slaughter is done 'humanely' – that is, quickly, painlessly and with minimal suffering to the animal. The *Shorter Oxford English Dictionary* defines 'humane' as 'characterised by such behaviour or disposition towards others as befits a man'. It adds descriptive words such as 'civil', 'kind' and 'benevolent'. In other words, we believe in treating animals with much the same compassion and dignity as we would hope to treat a fellow human being. So to regard people as animals is often to treat them worse than we treat animals.

We may not like to admit it, but we're all fragile in body and mind. Our bodies crumble through disease. We feel pain, we cry, we grieve. People also have potential; they are capable of great achievements. People are important whether they are keeping the streets clean or directing the affairs of state. They're precious. They're not even *merely* animals. However closely related we may be genetically to the animal kingdom, in biblical terms we are made in the image of God. We have certain characteristics that separate us from the rest of the living creatures.

Ultimately, that has to do with being capable of self–reflection and with building relationships with God and each other in complex human communities. However intelligent and capable of feeling animals may be, it is humans who have built elaborate cities and cultures and developed language to express abstract concepts and religious beliefs. It's humans who have invented complex machines, harnessed the power of the earth's resources, and greatly modified the environment (for better and for worse).

In dehumanising others we dehumanise ourselves. Something dies within us just as surely as discomfort, pain and even death is meted out to the victims. George Orwell captured this loss in the closing paragraph of his satire on collectivism, *Animal Farm*. 'The creatures outside looked from pig to man, and from man to pig, and from pig to man again; but already it was impossible to say which was which.'[28]

Remember that when you're next tempted to call someone a pig or a dog, or to refer to the drunken youths running riot in your town as 'pond life'. They're not. They're people, behaving badly, perhaps, but people nonetheless. Under the surface, they're just like you. And there are complex reasons for the way they act, but usually we're too busy, too unconcerned, to find out what these might be.

Before we leave this, there are two instances in the gospels where Jesus seems to denigrate people as animals. He once referred to the corrupt, hypocritical puppet king Herod as 'that fox',[29] and this is almost certainly a term of dismissive, perhaps prophetic, contempt. In Jewish culture at the time, to call a person a fox was to describe them as sly and worthless. When Jesus later came before Herod, on trial for his life, he maintained a stony silence,[30] suggesting that he regarded the ruler's questions as insincere mockery, and treated them with the dignified contempt they deserved.

The second instance was when Jesus was pestered by a Gentile (Canaanite) woman to heal her daughter. He ignored her at first, and said he was sent 'only to the lost sheep of Israel'. When she persisted, he added, 'It is not right to take the children's bread and toss it to the dogs.' He used the word for domestic pets, not wild dogs, but the point was the same: Jews regarded Gentiles as 'dogs' and had as little to do with them as possible. On this occasion, however, Jesus seems to be using the common belief in Jewish racial superiority as a device to draw out the woman's faith and to make a point to the bystanders in terms they could all understand, rather than to treat her with contempt. She responds, 'Yes it is, Lord, [but] even the dogs eat the crumbs that fall from their master's table.' She recognises him as the Saviour who knows no such distinction, and he heals the girl.[31] You don't do that if you find the person contemptible.

Isolated incidents like these must be put into the context of the whole Jesus story. His life was one of respect and inclusion. He did what to others seemed unthinkable things: he talked to a Samaritan woman he met at a well; he welcomed non-Jews who came to see him; he listened patiently to an old woman's medical history while on his way to deal with an emergency; and he rebuked people who tried to stop children coming up to him for a prayerful blessing.[32] He touched lepers (to most people, that seemed like risking contamination); and he took the servant's place to wash his disciples' feet, explaining that this was exactly how he expected his followers to act.[33] These are not the actions of a man proud of his race, pernickety in his habits, protective of his status. Rather they were the actions of someone who accepted all people whatever their reputation or situation. He put faces on the faceless, and gave dignity to the despised. He set the standard for human relationships.

Which, sadly, is regularly forgotten by internet trolls and headline-chasing media moguls, whose bad habits are far more contagious than Ebola.

The toll of the trolls

Barely a week goes by without some widely publicised example of extreme trolling in social media. People who often hide behind anonymity – deliberately making themselves faceless – post hate-filled messages, or start false rumours, aimed at people in the public eye or others whom they just dislike. Trolling forms a big part of bullying in schools, colleges and workplaces.

UK law is only slowly catching up with this menace, and in any case is a blunt instrument which few individuals have the time or money to wield effectively. The Defamation Act (2013) now requires claimants to show actual or probable 'serious harm', a much stricter rule than in the past and which has led to a fall in claims. Threats to life or messages of racial or religious hatred can be dealt with under other laws and have been pursued successfully in the courts – so long as the troll can be traced.

The hurt caused to victims and their families is well documented. The writer and political campaigner Jemima Khan was named in an anonymous Twitter posting in 2011. It alleged that she had had an affair with the TV presenter Jeremy Clarkson, which was the subject of a super-injunction.

Both allegations were false. Ms Khan was understandably furious. She publicly complained that as a result of the allegation she was receiving hate mail, and that her sons were liable to be bullied at school.

Kathy Sierra, an American computer programmer and blogger, wrote an article on a technical website that incurred the wrath of trolls. People sent her death threats and posted doctored images of her as a sexually mutilated corpse. 'I'm at home, with the doors locked, terrified,' she wrote. 'I'm afraid to leave my yard. I will never feel the same. I will never be the same.'[34]

Something similar happened to British doctor Professor Simon Wessely, an expert on chronic fatigue syndrome (otherwise known as ME), whose work established the condition as a genuine ailment from which a third of his patients recovered after both physical and psychiatric treatment. It was the latter element that caused a troll uprising, falsely accusing him of claiming that ME 'is all in the mind', that is, not a 'real' ailment. In a newspaper interview, he said that he had felt safer when working in Iraq and Afghanistan with the military than he did in a civilian hospital in the UK. 'It's constant stalking, harassment, attempts at intimidation,' he said. 'I'm accused of calling ailing patients malingerers, neurotic cripples, of throwing boys into swimming pools, stealing things, of plagiarising, misconduct, falsifying data, being in league with Pharma or the lackeys of insurance agencies ... that everything I do is part of a vast conspiracy to deny the truth – all of which are grossly, professionally defamatory.'[35]

This is all sinister, vicious, and destructive. As the historian G. D. H. Cole put it in a poem, 'Civil Riot', in many quarrels 'ethics get forgot.'[36] So too do facts, and so does human decency and civility. The technical term for verbal expressions of hatred and derision is the circumstantial *ad hominem* argument. *Ad hominem* is Latin for 'against the person'. It accuses someone of hypocrisy or ridicules their opinions, not by countering their argument with facts but by deriding the person, by demonising them. Facts don't come into it. It's employed excessively by politicians and is a common ingredient in 'reality' TV shows and soap operas, so it's hardly surprising that the practice filters down to street level. TV drama wouldn't be drama if it didn't have spats, of course – it would be unwatchable – but over time familiarity with the genre may breed contempt of, or impatience with, gentler ways.

Extreme negativism is easy to employ and hard to resist. But often it has the effect only of reinforcing the feel-good factor of the speaker and their supporters. Thus it panders to pride, and excuses us from the more difficult task of engaging creatively and positively with whatever issues are at stake. It's a cheap form of rabble rousing that adds nothing to the sum of human knowledge or the growth of human understanding. It clouds the truth rather than unveiling it. It obscures the fact that the uniqueness of the human race is our ability to reason and to empathise, to think and feel our way into other people's points of view. That's something trolls just don't get.

US President Barack Obama explains, 'It's easy to make a vote on a complicated piece of legislation look evil and depraved in a thirty-second commercial, it's very hard to explain the wisdom of that same vote in less than twenty minutes.'[37] That's a sad commentary on civic and political processes, but not an excuse for verbal abuse.

Among the worst examples of *ad hominem* trolling are the vitriolic exchanges between Christians who differ over their interpretation of Scripture or understanding of theological concepts. Sadly, Lord Maurice Glasman wasn't exaggerating when he said that 'religious people hate each other more than they hate others'.[38]

Spats and splits divert energy and attention from the primary mission of the church, which is to bring good news by word and deed to the general public. They confirm in the public mind that religion is unrelated to real life and can therefore be safely ignored. There are better ways of handling disagreements, as we shall examine in the final chapter.

Canadian author Margaret Attwood caricatured such futile debate in her surreal novel *After the Flood*. In the midst of civil disorder she envisaged fringe cults 'trolling for souls in torment'. Among them, 'The Lion Isaiahists and the Wolf Isaiahists both preached on street corners, battling when they met: they were at odds over whether it was the lion or the wolf that would lie down with the lamb once the Peaceable Kingdom had arrived.'[39] (The allusion is to a prophecy in Isaiah, where the text suggests that in fact it will be both-and, not either-or.)

Before we leave this, let us note how the print and broadcast media can feed our gossip-hungry souls and further distort our understanding of reality. In 2012, the *Daily Mail* ran a story claiming that a quarter of all people claiming sickness benefit had a criminal record. In fact, a quarter of the whole UK population has a criminal record if you take into account parking and speeding fines. The claim was a smear on benefits claimants and was referred to as 'shocking' by the employment minister of the time. When repeated (verbally or online) it soon became 'fact' that 'most' claimants are criminals.[40] Distortions like that can linger on for years and become part of folklore that 'everyone knows'.

So once again we are faced with the simple question: how would you react if someone posted or said hateful things about you? Exaggeration is inexcusable; it is not, however, inexplicable. Prepare to be discomfited.

Playing the blame game

There are three interrelated and inescapable truths about the way every human mind works. One is that when something goes wrong we will attempt to push the blame on to someone else or on to adverse circumstances. We make excuses so that we shoulder minimum responsibility. We cannot bear to feel ourselves culpable, which is why many people find it so hard to fully own up to their mistakes.

Such a blame game is as old as the human race. In the Garden of Eden, smitten with a previously unknown sense of burning guilt for having breached God's command, Adam blames Eve for having tasted the forbidden fruit: she made me do it. Eve, in turn, blames the serpent, which morally as well as literally no longer has a leg to stand on.[41]

But the understandable buck-passing does not remove personal responsibility. Neither human needed to act as they did; either of them could simply have said 'no'. But they didn't, and they were scarred for life as a result, not because of God's capriciousness but because they reaped the unintended but inevitable consequences of their thoughtless actions.

The second truth is that we consider ourselves at least as good as, and usually better than, everyone else. So when someone does something wrong, whether by intent or through error, we're quick to condemn and scorn them. It's obvious to us what they should, or should not, have done. The trouble is, it wasn't necessarily obvious to them at the time, not least because our post-incident judgement has the added benefit of hindsight.

Martin Laird, a writer on prayer, observes, 'The jaws of our convictions lock so tightly around people that we actually think we know what life is like for them, what they really ought to do or think, as though we know their innermost hearts, as though we know only what God knows.'[42] That is why praying for people who offend us is likely to be more productive for everyone than slagging them off in social media.

And that was why Jesus so roundly condemned abusive anger, likening it to murder: 'You have heard that it was said to the people long ago, "You shall not murder, and anyone who murders will be subject to judgment." But I tell you that anyone who is angry with a brother or sister will be subject to judgment. Again, anyone who says to a brother or sister, "Raca," [a term of abuse] is answerable to the court. And anyone who says, "You fool!" [a term of contempt] will be in danger of the fire of hell.'[43]

Jesus was highlighting the psychological link between anger, hatred and murder. He's saying that dehumanising someone, treating them as contemptible, is equally wrong whether it's done with words or a weapon. It achieves nothing, except to bolster our inflated sense of superiority and to perpetuate the cycle of hatred. It's not as if we're squeaky clean ourselves.

That leads us to the third truth about our devious minds: we are often much harsher in our judgements on others than we are on ourselves, even when we recognise our own guilt. Social psychologist Cordelia Fine suggests, 'We are strangely blind to how the subtleties of other people's situations might affect them. Our sensitivity to the context, so sharply tuned when applied to ourselves, becomes sloppy and careless when we focus on others.'[44]

So, to press home our victim status or our moral superiority, we slip easily into ridicule, scorn, slander and negative gossip. In the blunt words of the Book of Proverbs, whoever does so 'is a fool'.[45] The reasons are not hard to find. Such actions are socially destructive: 'A perverse person stirs up conflict, and a gossip separates close friends.'[46] The prohibition on spreading slander is added to several of the Ten Commandments in one résumé of Israelite law, along with not withholding wages, not perverting justice, not hating people in one's heart, and not seeking revenge.[47] It is a serious social injustice.

In the more familiar world of the New Testament, the apostles, who themselves were no strangers to being on the receiving end of slander, were equally strident against it but also encouraged replacement therapy. 'Get rid of all bitterness, rage and anger, brawling and slander, along with every form of malice,' said St Paul. Instead, 'Be kind and compassionate to one another, forgiving each other, just as in Christ God forgave you.'[48]

There's a reason for seeking the replacement, he says in another letter. Negative attitudes towards people both hinder and contradict the renewing work of the Holy Spirit in a person's life.[49] We can't be transformed to be like Jesus if we willingly persist in behaving like the devil, who, of course, is described as 'the accuser' in Scripture.[50] And what is the carping criticism that trips so easily off our tongue but 'accusation'?

Nor can we really focus on and practise these higher values of human life if our souls are crippled by anger. It is widely recognised in the medical profession that anger and hatred can damage our well-being. Anger releases the stress hormones of adrenaline and cortisol, increases our blood pressure and may raise our temperature. As part of the flight or fight response to danger, anger rises quickly but subsides slowly. It can eat into us like acid into metal, and in the long term can trigger depression and anxiety. It is definitely not good for us.

It also affects people quite unconnected with the cause of our anger. 'Nothing annihilates an inhibition as irresistibly as anger does,' observed the pioneering psychologist William James.[51] In other words, we just let fly, regardless of the consequences. The more subtle effects of our anger on others have been demonstrated in social psychology experiments. In one, volunteers were divided into two groups. One group was shown a film of an unprovoked and savage attack designed to make them angry. The other group was shown a film of colours and shapes, designed to relax them.

Both groups were then given (in what they thought was an unrelated experiment) a series of negligence cases and asked to assess them. Some of the cases included details of mitigating circumstances such as a lack of training given to the accused. The angry volunteers were much harsher in their assessments than the calmer ones; they 'negligently ignored these niceties as they clumsily attempted to balance the scales of retributive justice'.[52] In assessing other people's negligence, they themselves were negligent.

It bears out what most of us know. We get short shrift from someone who ought to know and do better 'because they've had (or are having) a bad day'. Anger is like a mountain avalanche. It can gain pace and strength as it careers down the social slopes. If it's not good for us, it certainly isn't good for others.

Dealing with it is easier said than done, of course. But just recognising the symptoms and dangers is a good start. So is remembering that we don't know – can't know – why someone is as they are. They just are, and that is why Jesus

216

commended peacemakers as 'children of God'.[53] If we're on the receiving end, 'a gentle answer turns away wrath, but a harsh word stirs up anger. The tongue of the wise adorns knowledge, but the mouth of the fool gushes folly.'[54] Don't give the avalanche a push.

Anger management books and courses tackle what can be a deep-seated issue that isn't resolved by a few simple steps, and is beyond the scope of this book. However, there are some preliminary steps anyone can take when the red mist starts to descend:

- Don't react immediately. Give yourself time to think about what has happened or been said.

- Don't return like with like. It achieves nothing except to deepen the well of bitterness. (Besides, some trolls delight in provoking responses; that's why they do it. Why play their game?)

- When writing an email or letter response, sleep on it before posting it and ask for someone else's opinion on it first.

- You do not have to retweet or 'like' a claim you have seen; how do you know it's true, and what good will retweeting or 'liking' do anyway?

- Walk away (literally) from a confrontational situation that is getting out of hand, or take some exercise in the fresh air, a proven remedy for stress.

- Recognise the emotion of anger for what it is – a mental event that can be brought under your control if you want.

But whether anger, rumour-mongering, trolling, misrepresenting, depersonalising and the other Judas traps that we have looked at in this and previous chapters affect us

217

or are perpetrated by us, one thing remains clear: all of us need a mind-change. The unflattering conclusion of the Old Testament prophet Jeremiah that 'the heart is deceitful above all things and beyond cure' is modified in the New Testament by Paul's encouragement to 'be transformed by the renewing of your mind'.[55]

The way we view (and therefore relate to) people can change. That will make us happier and better people, benefit others and make our world a better place.

Let's see how this renewing of the mind can occur.

Notes

[1] Thomas à Kempis, *The Imitation of Christ*, tr. E.M. Blaiklock, Hodder & Stoughton, 1979, p.28.

[2] Malala Yousafzai with Christina Lamb, *I am Malala*, Phoenix, 2014. The quotation is from p.70, the examples from pp.70, 98, 252.

[3] Malcolm White, *Atrocitology*, Canongate, 2011, p.537.

[4] Galatians 3:28. One debate is recorded in Acts 15. Paul lists his own Jewish credentials in Galatians 1:13-14, and he condemned Peter for separating from Gentiles in Galatians 2:11-16.

[5] Cited by William Klassen, *Judas*, SCM Press, 1996, p.31.

[6] Both examples are cited by Peter Stanford, *Judas: The Troubling History of the Renegade apostle*, Hodder & Stoughton, 2015, p.112.

[7] The allegations were collated from ancient sources by Hyam Maccoby, *Judas Iscariot and the Myth of Jewish Evil*, The Free Press (US edition), 1992, p.83.

[8] Ibid.

[9] Ron Rosenbaum, *Explaining Hitler*, Macmillan, 1998, p.324.

[10] James 3:5-6.

[11] We ought to note, for the sake of honesty, that there is one occasion in the New Testament where St Paul quotes, with apparent approval, an unflattering generalisation about the people of Crete (Titus 1:12). He was human too. Elsewhere his comments about 'the Jews' or 'Israelites' are directed at beliefs, or the actions of leaders, rather than

at the race as a whole; he was thankful for his Jewish roots which ultimately led him to Christ, and remained deeply concerned for the Jews (Galatians 3:24; Romans 10:1-4).

[12] Jesus told Peter to mind his own business when the apostle asked about the future destiny of John in John 21:22. In Matthew 24:36 he said no one could know about the timing of the end of the world.

[13] John 17:12 (KJV; the term is translated 'the one doomed to destruction' in some versions); 2 Thessalonians 2:3.

[14] Luke 23:40-43.

[15] Biblically, hell can be defined as 'exclusion from God's presence'. Jesus described it in one parable as 'darkness' which is the opposite of the 'light' of God's presence (Matthew 22:13). There, people would experience 'weeping and gnashing of teeth' – standard images for sorrow and frustration. In another parable he used the image of 'the fire of hell' which in the original language was *Gehenna*, or the Valley of Hinnom, a smouldering rubbish tip outside Jerusalem where in the past children had been sacrificed (Matthew 18:8-9). While some believe that this is a literal forecast of an unending cremation for evildoers, the fact that Jesus is speaking in parables suggests that his description (and that of the imagery of a lake of fire in Revelation 20:14-15) may also be referring to the spiritual experience of burning anguish and frustration at missed opportunities. Over the past few decades a number of 'Bible-believing' writers, including Dr John Stott, have suggested that 'everlasting' may refer to the effect (that there is no way back), rather than to an unending experience. This is commonly called 'annihilation'. In other words, hell is a release into unconscious oblivion rather than committal into an unending experience of torture. It is self-exclusion from God's presence, which a merciful God accepts regretfully and minimises the conscious effect.

[16] In the early church a tradition emerged that Christ descended into hell between his death and resurrection, in order to release its captives. It's called 'the harrowing of hell' and has scant biblical justification save one verse in 1 Peter 3:19. Its meaning is disputed not least because 'spirits' is rarely used in the Bible to describe human beings, dead or alive. The Apostles' Creed clause, 'he descended into hell', is more correctly rephrased by modern versions as, 'he descended to the dead' – Hades, or the abode of the dead. It means he *died*, fully, and that his

death atoned for people in all eras, not necessarily that he preached the gospel to the people there, giving them a second chance of repentance.

[17] Manasseh's appalling reign is recorded in 2 Kings 21:1-18.

[18] Dante, *The Divine Comedy*, 'Hell', Canto 34.

[19] This is expressed in typically blunt terms in James 2:8-13. For the universality of sin see Romans 3:23-24 and 6:23.

[20] Ross Kemp, *Gangs*, Penguin Books, 2008, p.99.

[21] Christopher Browning, *Ordinary Men*, Penguin Books, 2001, p.127.

[22] Philip Zimbardo, *The Lucifer Effect*, Rider, 2009, p.187.

[23] Ibid., p.251.

[24] Reported by Celina Dunlop in *The Archive Hour*, BBC Radio 4, 15th March 2008.

[25] Cited in Zimbardo, *op. cit.*, pp.14-16.

[26] Quoted by Orlando Figes, *The Whisperers*, p.91.

[27] Cited in Zimbardo, *op. cit.*, p.352.

[28] George Orwell, *Animal Farm*, Penguin Books, 1951, p.120. A recent TV series, *Humans*, gave an interesting twist to this theme when some of the robotic humans (synths) employed as domestic servants proved to be reprogrammed people and began to remember their past feelings, emotions and freedoms. Telling who was who, and treating them accordingly, became more difficult.

[29] Luke 13:32.

[30] Luke 23:8-12.

[31] Matthew 15:21-28.

[32] In order: John 4:1-30; John 12:20-23; Luke 8:40-56; Matthew 19:13-15.

[33] Matthew 8:1-4; John 13:1-17.

[34] Recounted by Tim Adams, 'The Angry Brigade', *The Observer*, 24th July 2011.

[35] Interview with Stephanie Marsh, *The Times*, 6th August 2011.

[36] The full poem is in *The Oxford Book of Twentieth Century Verse*, Guild Publishing edn., 1987, p.262.

[37] Barack Obama, *The Audacity of Hope*, Canongate Books, 2008, p.132.

[38] Maurice Glasman, quoted in an interview with Michael Freedland, *The Times*, 9th July 2011.

[39] Margaret Atwood, *After the Flood*, Virago, 2009, p.47. The allusion is to Isaiah 11:6-9.

[40] Reported by Sue Marsh, *The Guardian (online)*, 24th July 2012.

[41] Genesis 3.

[42] Martin Laird, *Into the Silent Land*, Darton, Longman & Todd, 2006, p.124.

[43] Matthew 5:21-22.

[44] Cordelia Fine, *A Mind of its Own*, Icon Books, 2007, pp.62-63.

[45] Proverbs 10:18.

[46] Proverbs 16:28.

[47] See Leviticus 19. The long list of miscellaneous commands includes a few odd-sounding ones which some commentators have used as an excuse to dismiss the lot. But prohibitions on sowing two kinds of crop in the same field could lead to loss of fertility over time; weaving two fabrics together could be uncomfortable in a hot climate; and while selective livestock breeding was practised, mating different kinds of animals was probably associated with pagan cults. The weird commands may not be so bizarre after all. See R. K. Harrison, *Leviticus*, Tyndale Old Testament Commentaries, InterVarsity Press, 1980, pp.199f.

[48] Ephesians 4:31-32.

[49] Colossians 3:8-14.

[50] Revelation 12:10.

[51] William James, *The Varieties of Religious Experience*, Collins Fontana Books, 1960, p.262. The original content of the book was given as the Gifford Lectures in 1901-1902.

[52] Cited by Cordelia Fine, *op. cit.*, pp.56f.

[53] Matthew 5:9.

[54] Proverbs 15:1-2.

[55] Jeremiah 17:9; Romans 12:2.

Chapter 8
The courage to change our mind

So far we have considered how to recognise and avoid various Judas traps, and discovered some positive changes we can make in order to improve our lives and contribute to making the world a better place. Now we can review what we have discovered and draw the threads together. We shall explore what is different about a Christian mind or outlook, and look at some specific values that our world specially needs today.

Crow's Law: 'Do not think what you want to think until you know what you ought to know.'[1]

People who betray trust or act wrongly sometimes do so simply because they are confused. They're not thinking straight. They act impulsively, perhaps, without thinking about consequences. They may be distracted in some way and just do what seems like a good idea at the time.

Most of us know the experience of looking back on a decision or an action and asking ourselves, 'Why did I do that? What was I thinking of?' And we don't really have an answer. That was just where we were. Not everyone is coldly calculating, ruthlessly rational, all the time. We get sucked into a pattern of behaviour which evolves without us really noticing – until it's too late.

Christopher Andrew's trawl through the archives of the Security Service (MI5) uncovered the interview records of Michael Bettany, an MI5 officer who was convicted in 1984 of passing UK secrets to the Russians. Why he did so remained a mystery. There was no obvious or coherent reason for his actions.

'He was not … a committed pro-Soviet Communist,' says Andrew. '"There was no simple motive," he told his interrogators, "it was a cumulative process." He did not even appear particularly hostile to the Security Service.' Bettany confessed relatively easily. Perhaps, like Judas en route to Akeldama, he recognised that he had reached the sorry end of a confused career, and threw in the towel.[2]

Judas' state of mind may have been equally confused. Throughout this book we have explored factors that may have contributed to making him the person he was, and we have seen how similar factors can affect people today. Some of the specific suggestions about Judas are of course mutually exclusive. For example, there is good reason to think of him as a driven, obsessive person, but it is unclear which particular obsession of the several we have considered tipped him over the edge.

However, the broad factors are mutually *inclusive*; Judas was probably influenced by most if not all of them. We can't say he was motivated *only* by greed, or *only* by malice, or *only* by anything. Like the rest of us, he was a complex mixture of musings and motives.

At the end of the nineteenth century the then Dean of Canterbury, Frederic Farrar, wrote a life of Christ in which he tried to get into the mind of Judas. As well as listing the likely feelings of jealousy, poverty, disappointment and despair

Farrar also suggested that 'a turbid, confused chaos of sins was welling in the soul of Judas – malice, worldly ambition, theft, hatred of all that was good and pure, ingratitude, frantic anger ... all rushing with blind, bewildering fury through this gloomy soul'.[3]

Rushing, blind, bewildering, gloomy: that is not a good place to be. Perhaps being an energetic, intelligent, driven kind of person, anxious for acceptance, ambitious for himself, arrogant in his opinions, Judas lacked the self-awareness which in others might act as a brake on their potential excesses. Perhaps, if we had asked him, like Michael Bettany, he wouldn't know *precisely* why he betrayed Jesus.

Developing a Christian mind

In order to avoid falling into that kind of black hole, or into any of the more specific 'Judas traps', we need a framework for decision-making and for everyday living. We need to learn to think 'Christianly'. This is more than pasting a veneer of faith over a western lifestyle. It is a radically different, yet relatively simple, way of looking at and thinking about *everything*. It has six marks.

It is centred on the cosmic Christ

To be Christ-centred is more than being a committed church member. It is more than accepting that Christ's life provides us with a model to follow, or that his death atoned for our sins. It is more than asking what Jesus would do when we face a difficulty.

To be Christ-centred means acknowledging Jesus in all our activity for who he really was, is and ever shall be: the cosmic ruler of all that exists. Jesus was the full expression on earth of the eternal Godhead. Through him 'all things were created: things in heaven and on earth, visible and invisible, whether thrones or powers or rulers or authorities; all things have been created through him and for him.'[4] He designed everything from quantum particles to giant nebulae. He constructed the delicate ecosystem teeming with flora and fauna that we call home. Then he took a close and active interest in what people did in it and with it.

Seeing that we made a hash of it, this uncreated, limitless being willingly embraced the limitations of human birth, life and death. He did it to show us how he expected us to live, and to pave a new way to reunite us with himself. He did it out of sheer love for the world he had made. He walked where we walk, enjoyed as we enjoy, and suffered more than we are likely to suffer. God is love, not hate. God is for humanity, not against it. God has stooped low to save us from ourselves.

Christ's temporary human body, nailed to a Roman cross, was raised from death. It was transformed into the prototype of a renewed, re-formed humanity living in a dimension beyond the confines of the physical universe. It provided a glimpse into the mystery of life beyond death.

Now, moment by moment, 'in him all things hold together'; he is 'sustaining all things by his powerful word'. From the prophet Isaiah's soaring poetry depicting him as the never-wearying protector of the universe to Jesus' simple assertion that not a single sparrow falls to the ground without God's consent, the Bible tells us that God remains active in our universe.[5]

It is through Christ, the designer and keeper of what we call the laws of nature, that the sun keeps shining, the earth keeps turning, and we keep breathing and breeding. Nothing in the world, nothing in human affairs, nothing in an individual's life, is beyond his purview. Nothing that we do personally or corporately bores him; *everything* we do interests him intensely. Jesus Christ is Lord of every detail. The Christian mind never forgets that.

This is his world, not ours. We are the tenants, not the owners. We're here on borrowed time with a mandate to cooperate with God in renewing a world and community marred by imperfection at best and devastated by evil at worst.

He does not approve of all that people do, of course. He grieves over the blatant selfishness and evil which causes misery and suffering to millions. The cosmic Christ is no pushover. He is also the ultimate dispenser of justice. He will return to judge the world, which will be the end of time as we know it.

To those who asked why justice seems so long coming, Peter answered, 'The Lord is not slow in keeping his promise, as some understand slowness. Instead he is patient with you, not wanting anyone to perish, but everyone to come to repentance.' It can't be easy for him, holding on in the hope that prodigals will return.[6]

It acknowledges universal failure

The Bible's narrative is a list of failures and recoveries. That's probably the story of most people's lives, too. Yet we rarely follow Paul's instruction not to 'think of yourself more highly than you ought, but rather think of yourself with sober judgment'.[7] Generally we rate ourselves better than many others we can think of. When we fail to keep to our own high standards, well, everyone makes mistakes; it's only human nature. Others, though, are afforded less consideration when their failings impact on us.

The Christian mind is realistic about its own fallibility, mourns its frequent sins and accepts that we cannot expect perfection from others either. 'All have sinned and fall short of the glory of God,' explained Paul. But in calling for realism, he also countered despair. He continued, 'and all are justified freely by his grace through the redemption that came by Christ Jesus.'[8] From the ashes of sin there can arise a saint.

'Know thyself' was engraved on the wall of the ancient Greek temple in Delphi, the seat of the fabled oracle. To assess ourselves realistically is a powerful challenge. So too is the wry observation of actor and TV personality Stephen Fry: 'The mask if worn long enough will be the face.'[9] We put a mask over our true self and believe its myths about our moral and spiritual rectitude. We forget that a divine eye peers into the dark corners of our personality, and seeks to enlighten them.

Human failure does not consist only of the lapses we know about. There is also the uncomfortable fact that we are born selfish. It's partly a survival instinct, a protective reflex – a crying baby cannot be comforted until fed – but it can turn later into a drive for power and gain which we find hard to resist.

This natural bias is what Christian theology calls 'original sin', and what King David meant when he confessed 'I was sinful at birth'.[10] We can and do achieve great things and do much good. But we can never quite match up to the absolute perfection that is required of is.

We can't even rely on that inner voice we call conscience to keep us on the straight and narrow. True, we are hard-wired with an innate awareness that there are such things as right and wrong, true and false. The trouble is, conscience can easily be manipulated. Paul encountered people whose consciences were corrupted, or cauterised as with a hot iron.[11]

Reviewing the Bolshevik revolution in Russia during the 1930s, historian Orlando Figes discovered that 'communist morality left no room for the western notion of the conscience as a private dialogue with the inner self'. Rather, the Russian word for 'conscience' was replaced by another with the idea of 'the capacity to reach a higher moral judgement' – that is, to agree with whatever conformed to party policy at the time. A true Bolshevik 'would be ready to believe that black was white and white was black, if the Party required it'.[12]

This helps to explain why some people feel no pangs of conscience when they break laws. Their actions seem fine to them. Theft, corruption, murder, even genocide can be justified by arguments, but that doesn't make them right. Nor does the common excuse for petty cheating: 'Everybody does it.'

The Greek word for conscience in the New Testament literally means 'to know with someone'. It implies that conscience only functions accurately when it is informed by a higher standard than our own knowledge or culture. So we find that not even Paul trusted it. 'My conscience is clear,' he told the Corinthian church, 'but that does not make me innocent. It is the Lord who judges me.'[13]

There are genuine grey areas, too; one Christian's conscience will allow them to do something (say, work on a Sunday) which others believe is wrong. Paul had a major conscience issue to deal with in the churches. Some people felt that eating meat (the slaughter of which was usually accompanied by pagan rituals) was wrong. It did not affect the cardinal truths about the person and work of Christ. However, although Paul himself would eat anything, he recognised the need not to offend those who wouldn't by flouting his freedom.[14]

It is bounded by truth

Truth is sometimes considered to be a relative quality rather than an absolute standard. That is, what is true for me may not be true for everyone. Thus truth can be bent to fit an agenda.

In 2007 the public relations trade magazine *PR Week* ran a debate on the motion 'PR has a duty to tell the truth'. It was narrowly lost by 138 votes to 124. Speakers against the motion spoke of the 'soothing effect' of lies. Those for the motion warned that lying creates 'a world that has been based on posturing'.[15]

Five years later, Essex University launched a Centre for the Study of Integrity, itself noteworthy: if integrity needs studying, something is amiss. In a survey it found that people were becoming more tolerant of dishonesty. 'Only 33 per cent of under-25s thinks lying on a job application is never justified, compared with 41 per cent of middle-aged people and 55 per cent of those over 65,' it found.[16]

The reason we lie is, at root, very simple. The author Dorothy Rowe says, 'Every lie we tell, no matter how small and unimportant, is a defence of our sense of being a person.' Her ominous conclusion is that 'in the world we live in, truth is always revolutionary'.[17]

Christians can dispense with defensiveness. We can afford, like our founder, to be revolutionary. Jesus claimed that he *was* the truth – the embodied truth about the character of God. He said that the nature of the Holy Spirit, the motivator and guide for Christian living, is truthfulness and that his function is to reveal error and teach truth.[18] No room for approximation there.

Jesus also told religiously orthodox people that 'the truth will set you free'.[19] He was referring to freedom from the slavish adherence to religious rules and rituals that held them back from entering and enjoying a more direct, personal relationship with God. Religion can enslave rather than liberate. Its disciplines may provide a helpful structure for worship and discipleship, but they are not to be mistaken for worship and discipleship themselves.

Commentator William Barclay helpfully suggested that discipleship – the process of allowing Christ to transform our minds and reform our actions – resulted in four freedoms. There is freedom from fear (Jesus is always with us); freedom from ourselves (Jesus can forgive and revitalise us); freedom from other people (especially from anxiety about what they might think, say or do); and freedom from sin: 'Discipleship breaks the chains which bind us to our sins, and enables us to be the person we know we ought to be.'[20]

This implies that all who seek to follow God are to be scrupulously honest. 'Each of you must put off falsehood and speak truthfully to your neighbour, for we are all members of one body,' Paul wrote. He was echoing an earlier prophet who said, '"Speak the truth to each other, and render true and sound judgment in your courts; do not plot evil against each other, and do not love to swear falsely. I hate all this," declares the Lord.'[21]

That, of course, is little more than common sense. Lies breed trouble. Dorothy Rowe comments, 'If you must lie to others, do it knowing that you are lying, and be aware that there will be unintended and unimagined consequences. Never lie to yourself. If you do you will never be able to escape the terrible consequences.'[22]

Someone who discovered that to his cost was Jonathan Aitken. He was Minister of State for Defence, and later Chief Secretary to the Treasury, in John Major's government in the early 1990s. Newspaper articles accused him of corruption, which he vigorously defended in a libel case. In doing so, he lied in court. 'I needed to present a seamless web of rebuttal,' he wrote later. 'If that meant telling a lie about the relatively unimportant matter of who paid my £900 Ritz Hotel bill, it seemed to me to be a necessary small one in self-defence against much greater falsehoods.'[23]

That one small lie lost him his career, and cost him a prison sentence for perjury. Small lies, the ones we call 'white' (there are no such grades of lies in Scripture) are as much a betrayal of truth as large ones. If we want to spare someone pain, there are ways of responding gently without lying. Truth does not have to be blunt.

It also follows that if God *is* truth, then there are also universal, or absolute, truths that define what is right and wrong in both belief and conduct. 'What is truth?' Pontius Pilate asked Jesus dismissively – a very modern response when faced with conflicting beliefs.[24] Agnosticism is preferred to assertion.

Christian faith rests on 'revealed' truths. If there is a God, then it's likely that he would make some form of self-disclosure so that we could know who he is and what he expects of us. Rather than force us to believe, he has revealed just enough for us to 'seek him and perhaps reach out for him and find him, though he is not far from any one of us,' as Paul said to the sceptical philosophers in Athens.[25] He encourages faith rather than enforces obedience.

'In the past God spoke to our ancestors through the prophets at many times and in various ways, but in these last days he has spoken to us by his Son,' begins the letter to the Hebrews.[26] Jesus is the most complete self-disclosure of God that could be imagined: God himself in human form. We have reliable information about who Jesus was, what he said and did, and the purpose and meaning of his crucifixion and

231

resurrection. God has provided a framework of truth in the Scriptures and the life of Jesus. He has not left us to flounder in total spiritual darkness.

But there is a snag. Some truths about God are unfathomable in their entirety; the human mind cannot grasp them fully. Christians may differ over what is absolute truth and what in the Bible is a cultural concession (the issue of whether women can be church leaders is one). Sometimes they have to agree to disagree. That may sound like having our cake and eating it. It can open Christians to the charge of intellectual laziness. However, Christian experience down the ages provides sufficient assurance that in practice the basic truths of God and Christ, summarised in the creeds, can be trusted. The Christian mind trusts that God knows more than we do.

It is directed by humanitarian concern

Altruism doesn't come easily or naturally. We may make big sacrifices for our family and modest ones for our closest friends, but only occasionally will we put ourselves out for total strangers (unless we work for the emergency services).

Paul knew this as he meditated on the depths of Christ's love: 'Very rarely will anyone die for a righteous person, though for a good person someone might possibly dare to die. But God demonstrates his own love for us in this: while we were still sinners, Christ died for us.'[27] (The distinction between 'righteous' and 'good' cannot be pressed, other than to suggest tentatively that 'good' may refer to someone who is both morally upright and inspires affection.)

Altruism, though, is what Scripture expects. Jesus said that there are two chief commandments: to love God with one's heart, soul, mind and strength – that is, to centre our whole life on him – and to love our neighbour as ourselves, which

232

means in equal measure.[28] Their welfare is as important as ours. Showing love to them is as important as offering worship to God.

George Orwell's satirical novel *Animal Farm* depicts animals taking over the business. There, 'no creature called any other creature "Master". All animals were equal.' So far, so biblical. Jesus envisaged the Christian community operating in similar egalitarian ways: don't call one another 'master', 'father' or 'teacher', he said, because 'you are all brothers' and 'you have one Instructor, the Messiah'. Paul's description of the church as the 'body of Christ' shows each member having equally valued, if noticeably different, functions.[29]

Towards the end of Orwell's story, things changed. Some animals began walking on two legs, proclaiming their higher status. Then a new commandment replaced the earlier rules on the farmyard wall: 'All animals are equal but some are more equal than others.'[30]

Orwell was reflecting on the descent of communist idealism into a totalitarian dictatorship. But there seems to be a law of social entropy affecting all cultures. Good intentions of fairness and compassion disintegrate into self-serving divisions and power seeking. In a crisis we may pull together. In normal times it's everyone for themselves.

People matter more than things. If God loves all people and gave himself for them, then so should we. And not in the sense of 'I love mankind; it's people I can't stand', either. We have to relearn how to treat other people as if they were members of our own family.

It has a global perspective

In practice, we tend to restrict our expression of humanitarian concern to situations known to us personally or featured in charity appeals such as Sport Relief or Children in Need. The Christian mind knows no such limitations. God loves the world that we fail to see.

We live in a global village. The world has shrunk through travel and television. We can see personally or virtually that people in vastly different cultures, climates and conditions are just like us in many ways. They breed, and bleed. They laugh, and cry. They work, and play.

We forget how interconnected we are. The supermarket shelves bulge with goods sourced from across the globe, but apart from perhaps looking for a Fairtrade logo, we barely give their origins a second thought. Many of our clothes, vehicles and household appliances are made in one country using materials from several others.

God's creation mandate was for human beings to 'fill the earth and subdue it'.[31] It was an instruction to nurture the physical, animal and plant worlds responsibly on behalf of the Creator and for the benefit of all. It was not given so that oil giants, logging companies and farming conglomerates could trash tribal lands and animal habitats as they have in parts of Africa, Asia and South America. Nor was it permission to consume resources in such a manner that we hastened the melting of ice caps, the rising of sea levels and the desertification of once productive forest or farmland. Human nature being what it is, alarm bells start to ring when we hear reports that the architecture of Venice is in danger of sinking beneath the waves, but not when it is suggested that the delta-dwelling people of Bangladesh are in mortal peril from the encroaching ocean.

It is fair to assume that God is not pleased by thoughtless exploitation of the world he endowed us with, merely to fuel, feed and clothe a disproportionately rich third of the population. A Christian mind takes global responsibility seriously.

The Christians in Antioch, the capital of Syria and the third largest city in the Roman Empire, were warned of an impending food crisis in Judea 500 kilometres to the south. They understood their responsibilities, and 'decided to provide help for the brothers', using Barnabas and Paul (still called Saul at that time) as couriers.[32]

The early church wasn't always so generous in its foreign aid, though. Paul had to urge the southern Greek church of Corinth to emulate its northern Greek counterpart (Macedonia) and complete a collection for the beleaguered church in Jerusalem. The Macedonians had also been consistently supportive of Paul himself, an early example of a church putting a missionary on its charitable giving list.[33]

Jesus also commanded: 'Go and make disciples of all nations, baptising them in the name of the Father and of the Son and of the Holy Spirit, and teaching them to obey everything I have commanded you.'[34] This mission mandate urges Christians to proclaim of the good news of Jesus. But 'making disciples' envisages more than saving souls or increasing church attendance.

Catholic missionary Vincent Donovan described a radical rethink of Christian mission to the Masai peoples of Africa. He claimed that 'only Christianity has the inherent capacity' to unite nations and 'the inner strength necessary to match the primeval force of racism and tribalism'.[35] Christian mission has world-saving potential.

Jesus broke down racial and cultural barriers. He talked to a Samaritan woman, and he healed a Canaanite girl and a Roman centurion's servant.[36] The early church took a while to grasp this. There was fierce debate about the legitimacy of Gentile conversions if they did not also include the adoption of Jewish cultural practices. Yet within two decades of Jesus' death, Paul was confidently writing that 'there is neither Jew nor Gentile, neither slave nor free, nor is there male and female, for you are all one in Christ Jesus'.[37]

Unfortunately that principle can be forgotten when national, political, racial or other interests take hold. Apartheid in South Africa was given a spurious 'Christian' justification, resulting in non-white peoples being oppressed and exploited rather than welcomed and valued. Today in many localities churches collaborate to support counselling centres and foodbanks, united services or walks of witness and Christian Aid collections. This, and the personal injection of Christian values into workplaces and communities by individual Christians, is a valuable part of mission.

But actively promoting Christian faith in a multicultural global village can be low on the agenda. Loud voices in society claim religious beliefs are a private matter, and Christians can be cowed into silence. Different religions are generally considered to be of equal value whatever they teach or believe.

'Missionary work' overseas is criticised for allegedly exporting or imposing a narrow culture. Evangelistic events may be denounced as 'emotional' or superficial. Proselytising is frowned upon. Churches then become inward-looking, guarding their culture, customs and worship styles but playing down disciple-making.

There have been abuses, lessons are there to be learned, and wisdom and sensitivity need to be exercised. But they do not alter the mandate to make disciples – followers of Jesus who in turn discover how God can transform their lives and values. Christianity is a missionary faith, by order of its founder. It has good news to share. The Christian mind cannot ignore the call.

As Jesus surveyed the cultural, religious and commercial capital of his own small country, and wept over it, we can mourn the moral and spiritual poverty of our society. But after the tears must come the pledge to put the physical, moral and spiritual well-being of all peoples before our own interests.[38]

It keeps everything in perspective

When Moses asked God what his name was, he was given an enigmatic response: 'I AM WHO I AM'.[39] Jesus applied that name to himself in his most overt claim to divinity: 'Before Abraham was born, I am!' His critics had no doubt what he meant and attempted to stone him, the traditional death penalty for blasphemy.[40]

It just means 'God lives', beyond the bounds of time, spanning eternity. In the Bible, 'eternity' means 'long ages', an infinite extension of time in all directions. Space- and time-bound humans have no other categories to conceive it, but we can dispense with our concept of linear time altogether and think instead about a continuous present.

Recall those moments when time has stood still. Absorbed in a hobby or project, or exploring and contemplating a scene, we lose all sense of passing time. Think back to childhood or observe young children for whom time is a foreign concept. The past is forgotten; the future is unimaginable. All that exists is the present moment. We just *are*. Life just *is*. It's only as we grow older that we become aware of the number of sleeps we have to endure before Christmas.

God is not constrained by time. God is, as he was, and ever shall be long after the sun becomes a red giant and the earth dies. God does not measure time by the rotations of the earth or its revolutions around the sun. In the biblical imagery of God's eternal dimension that we call heaven, there is no sun, just the divine radiance that never dims. Hence 'a thousand years in your sight are like a day that has just gone by'.[41]

That is why it's so spiritually (and psychologically) unhelpful to keep beating ourselves up over past failures and sins. God, in his eternal present, does not have a 'past', so he doesn't keep looking back to ours. He has accepted our confession and appeal to the death of his Son for forgiveness, and focuses on our present. He is interested in what we do with our today. His message is for now: there is work only you can do.

It challenges our frantic rush, too. 'Life's short; let's live it well' was the running strapline of a short-lived UK newspaper, *The New Day*, launched in 2016. It's a useful reminder that life is not to be wasted, and with that the apostles concur. Paul's encouragement to Christian living was, 'Be very careful, then, how you live – not as unwise but as wise, making the most of every opportunity, because the days are evil.'[42]

However, we're not expected to cram as much as we can into our days, or fulfil a bucket list of 'must do' visits, experiences and tasks. The Christian mind accepts that we can't do everything and seeks instead to serve God and the community with our current skills and resources day by day.

As Paul approached the end of his life, he told one of his protégés; 'I have fought the good fight, I have finished the race, I have kept the faith. Now there is in store for me the crown of righteousness.'[43] In God's eternal present, there is no end to life. It will go on. The resurrection of Jesus, destroying the stranglehold of death, was the tangible sign that his promise that 'whoever believes in him shall not perish but have eternal life'[44] was not given in vain.

The mind can be remoulded

We can use these six marks of a Christian mind as a checklist against which to measure our views, attitudes, decisions and actions about anything and everything. They may help us to avoid the Judas traps.

- Is my attitude or action consistent with the character and purposes of Jesus Christ, the unchanging Lord of the universe, and with my commitment to him as his disciple?

- Is my attitude or action taking full account of my own inherent imperfection and the likely human weaknesses of others?

- Is my attitude or action compliant with all that is true, in terms both of honesty in thought and deed and of the known truth about God and his requirements?

- Is my attitude or action likely to help or hinder other people's lives, feelings and view of God through me, and what effect might it have on someone who is especially vulnerable?

- Is my attitude or action taking account of its likely impact on the environment and on the physical and spiritual welfare of people beyond my own shores, whom God also loves and cares about?

- Is my attitude or action being hurried by my impatience or tempered by my trust in God's good purposes in the eternal 'now' in which time is not an issue?

This is somewhere to start, but unfortunately, we can still mess up. We can pay lip service to one or more of these marks while pursuing our own agenda. That *is* human nature! We need not just a change of mind, but a new mind. The Bible says we can have one.

Paul urged the Romans not to be conformed to the thinking habits of the general public but to 'be transformed by the renewing of your mind'. Translator J. B. Phillips rendered the passage thus: 'Don't let the world around you squeeze you into its own mould, but *let God re-mould your minds from within*, so that you may prove in practice that the plan of God for you is good, meets all his demands and moves towards the goal of true maturity.'[45]

Paul declared that since the resurrection of Christ, God has 'put his Spirit in our hearts'. Christians are (or can be) a 'new creation' in whom 'the old has gone, the new is here'. It is this transformation that is envisaged in the sometimes misunderstood term about being 'born again'.[46]

Christian faith is not merely an intellectual philosophy, not just a rule of life, but it is intended to be a dynamic partnership with the living God. This results in a slowly evolving change of attitudes and priorities (sometimes called 'sanctification'). It is a cooperative adventure, not a diktat from headquarters. God never overrides the individual's will. 'Work out your salvation with fear and trembling,' writes Paul, 'for it is God who works in you to will and to act in order to fulfil his good purpose'.[47]

So if you don't fancy having your mind remoulded from within, you don't have to. But you won't get far in the Christian life – and you will be more likely to mess up – unless you do. This transformation won't turn you into Superman or Superwoman, nor will you become the caricature Holy Joe that we all love to hate. God made you as you are; he just wants you to be a better you.

It is a lifelong progression. Even Paul continually struggled with his 'old self'. Christian faith is not a quick fix for anything. He reminded the Colossians that in coming to Christ they had 'put on the new self, which is being renewed in knowledge in the image of its Creator'. They would never be quite the same again. Yet they still had to rid themselves of shortcomings such as lust and greed, malice and slander.[48] Only in heaven will the transformation be complete.

While this is an essentially 'spiritual' occurrence, we saw in chapter 4 that it's not entirely without a rational and scientific basis. The brain, and its countless connections, are not so fixed that they cannot be altered. A person's outlook can be modified over time as the result of an appropriate therapy or medical intervention. The rainy outlooks of severely depressed people can become brighter and less gloomy, if not always sunny.

However, this spiritual process of remoulding is not an alternative to professional treatment for severe mental illness or neurological disorders. Christian faith may well be an important contributory factor in any healing process. But the damage which can be been done to some people by zealous advocates of purely spiritual remedies, who underestimate the complexities of the whole person, is deeply regrettable.

Now take a deep breath.

Stop and listen

One way to avoid messing up is to stop what we're doing and think. American spirituality writer Robert Wicks observes that 'we rush around like a gargoyle on roller skates, while failing to notice people we have hurt, what we are eating, how we are feeling, or even what we are really doing'.[49] If our life is like that then we are most at risk of messing up. At the very least, we're not living well.

Oxford Professor Mark Williams recounts an experiment by an American psychologist. An actor stopped people in the street to ask for directions. During the conversation two other people carrying a door came between them. In that instant, the actor was switched with another. When the door had passed by, only about half the members of the public noticed that they were instructing a completely different person.[50] It was a graphic demonstration of the way many of us go through life on autopilot. We become absorbed in our private worlds, submerged under pressured demands. The continuous current of thoughts and concerns sweeps away the 'still dews of quietness' that might otherwise make us more aware of the world above the churning waves.

We need to stop in order to be still. We need to be still in order to listen. We need to listen in order to better understand ourselves, to hear God's quiet voice addressing us, and to allow him the time to remould our minds. Many people are afraid of silence because it amplifies aloneness. It allows buried memories and fears to bubble to the surface. We use the radio, TV or iPod to drown out the inner murmurs.

Author and professor C. S. Lewis addressed the issue of noise and silence more than once. In the humorous and perceptive *The Screwtape Letters* the senior devil tells a junior demon that noise is a key ingredient in their battle to distract and divert Christians from God's path: 'We will make the whole universe a noise in the end … The melodies and silences of Heaven will be shouted down in the end.'[51] In his sci-fi novel *Voyage to Venus*, written during the chaos and cacophony of the Second World War, Lewis described his hero Professor Ransom trying to focus on the unseen but awesome presence of the great spirit Maleldil. 'Inner silence is for our race a difficult achievement. There is a chattering part of the mind which continues, until it is corrected, to chatter even in the holiest places.'[52]

To us, silence is an absence of something reassuring. Yet silence brings us into the far more reassuring presence of God. As three disciples blethered about erecting shelters on the Mount of Transfiguration, having had a literally out-of-this-world experience with Jesus, the voice of God hit them like a thunderclap: 'This is my Son, whom I love. Listen to him!'[53]

Listen! We say it to fretful or demanding children focused solely on their fear or frustration. Listen! There's a reason why we must do this or can't do that. But fretful or demanding children are not open to such adult reasoning. They can't understand it.

Listen! God says when his fretful or demanding children are focused solely on their latest desire or raging against some inconvenience or injustice. Listen! But we can't listen when we're racing ahead or stamping our feet. We can't understand divine ways.

How do you listen to God? There's no technique involved; just patience. The more we listen, the more we learn to listen. The key is to set time aside, not for a hurried thought for the day (although that is not to be despised when coping with the heavy demands of family and career). Rather we need to find unhurried time, as Jesus did when he went off away from the crowds to pray alone.

In silence, we can meditate. Swiss doctor and spiritual writer Paul Tournier wrote, 'Meditation leads to the discovery of one's true self and to self-confidence. It gives one a clear vision of what he has that he can share with others, and heals his fear so that his own worth is affirmed at the same time that he is led into a positive attitude toward the rest of the community.'[54] In other words, it's not an escape from life but an equipping for it.

Today, Christians are rediscovering meditation as an aid to spiritual growth. It even has more than just spiritual benefits. 'Many people find that blood pressure decreases or stabilises, the pulse slows down, and there is greater emotional tone,' claims Christian meditation teacher Martin Laird, adding that 'we get over things more quickly.'[55] What's not to like about that?

How do we meditate? We can use a word or short phrase from the Bible to help us focus on the ever-presence of God. We allow the mind to quieten down, and we shelve the inevitable wandering thoughts, to pick them up later. The purpose is just to be, in God's presence, who can then set our concerns in a wider perspective.

Or we can read a Bible passage reflectively. That means slowly, preferably aloud, and several times. Sometimes a word or an idea will seem to be especially important, and we can allow it to teach us about anything on God's agenda. We can't expect him to tell us only what we want to hear.

Just as important as listening to God is listening to other people. Indeed, God will often speak to us through other people's counsel. That's why it's important to share ideas and plans with others, something that Judas apparently failed to do.

Just as we tend to rush into God's presence with a shopping list of needs, so we can be equally impatient with others. We offer solutions before we know the real questions. We 'hear what you say' but never stop to explore why you hold that opinion, and where you are coming from. 'Everyone should be quick to listen, slow to speak and slow to become angry,' counselled the apostle James.[56]

Sometimes, people don't want our answers. They just need a listener. Sharing a burden with another person is often help enough. But who has time to listen, not offering hasty comment but giving compassionate empathy? 'Even fools are thought wise if they keep silent, and discerning if they hold their tongues,' a wise man said long ago.[57]

There are some ground rules. Chief among them is keeping confidences. We love knowing something others do not, and the temptation is always to pass it on. For all the concern today for 'transparency', releasing personal information into the public domain (even if that domain is a couple of 'trusted' friends) is a betrayal, unless the person sharing it has given us permission to do so for a specific reason.

We also have a responsibility not to spread or elaborate gossip, one of eight unpleasant traits that were damaging the fellowship and witness of the Corinthian church.[58] I once worked on an inter-church outreach mission that was almost halted because a member of the organising committee had heard from someone else that the invited speaker had left his wife for another woman. There wasn't a shred of truth in it, but the gossiper took some convincing. Why do we always believe the worst?

If we hear something about another person which disturbs us, Jesus implied that we should check its veracity down the chain.[59] But then, when do we ever have time or inclination to do that? Juicy gossip is more fun than patient research.

So stop, be still, listen, and...

Be thankful

In a frenetic society we easily lose our sense of appreciation and wonder. We have so much, compared with poorer people in our own community and those who have little or nothing in refugee camps and the slums, shanties and subsistence villages of the two-thirds world.

We saw in chapter 5 that we could counter the grip of materialism by contentment and generosity. The key to finding contentment, and the source of generosity, is gratitude. It does not come easily. We need to learn again to say thank you. But not just in the way of a courteous card or letter after a party or a gift. Gratitude more than that. It is a way of rejoicing that reduces, and in time removes, our untransformed instinct to grasp and possess.

In Daniel Defoe's eighteenth-century novel *Robinson Crusoe*, based loosely on a real incident, the eponymous castaway was stranded on a desert island. After about three years he realised that there was more than enough on the island to sustain him indefinitely. Defoe has him reflect, 'I learned to look on the bright side of my condition, and less upon the dark side, and to consider what I enjoyed, rather than what I wanted [that is, lacked]'.[60] His gratitude and contentment made the privations of his life bearable, even enjoyable.

Gratitude can have a healing effect. Ten men suffering from a skin disease came to Jesus for healing. They were outcasts because of other people's fears of being contaminated. Jesus received them, just as he received others shunned by society, and gave them what they asked for. Their dignity restored, they raced off rejoicing like a syndicate that has just won the lottery, able to take their place in the community once more.

Then one came back. He was the lone foreigner in the group. He said thank you to Jesus and expressed praise to God. To him alone, Jesus said, 'your faith has made you well' – literally, 'saved you'.[61] His gratitude brought him a spiritual enrichment of life that exceeded even the new possibilities that his physical healing offered.

Gratitude opens our heart to God. It helps to unblock the channels through which the renewing Holy Spirit can flow. 'It is probable that in most of us the spiritual life is impoverished and stunted because we give so little place to gratitude,' wrote William Temple, a former Archbishop of Canterbury. 'It is more important to thank God for blessings received than to pray for them beforehand.' Gratitude, he adds, is quite selfless and 'akin to love'.[62]

The early twentieth-century Christian author and journalist G. K. Chesterton went further: 'I would maintain that thanks are the highest form of thought; and that gratitude is happiness doubled by wonder.'[63]

It is no surprise, then, that spiritual teachers encourage the regular habit of thanksgiving. Paul said that it should always be associated with prayers and petitions, thereby making us receptive to 'the peace of God, which transcends understanding'.[64] Some suggest finding ten things (one for each finger) to say thank you for at the end of each day. If that seems hard, try one hand first.

Had a bad day? Here are ten things you could be grateful for that are probably unrelated to it. You will notice that some of them are really several things bound together, so the list could be longer.

1. The roof over your head.
2. The items in your room or home that contribute to your comfort.
3. The materials the objects are made from, the people who sourced them and those who designed and manufactured them.
4. The clothes on your back and in your wardrobe, and the raw materials they are made from.
5. The people who grew and made the raw materials and designed, made and cut the fabrics.

6. The energy that powers the lights and appliances, charges your phone, fuels your car, bus or train, and the people who maintain the supply.
7. The food you have eaten today; the shops where it was bought; the manufacturers who processed it; the farmers who produced it; the entire supply chain.
8. The trees, plants, even the weeds sprouting on waste land, the birds in the air – all natural things that beautify the world and are vital components of the ecosystem on which we depend.
9. Your friends and family, and all that they contribute to your sense of well-being.
10. Jesus, whose life, death, resurrection and ascension are the source of eternal forgiveness, renewal and hope.

Once we're listening carefully, and becoming grateful, then we'll start minding our language.

Speak and act graciously

If we ever needed proof of the transformation of Saul of Tarsus from fire-breathing, venom-spitting scourge of Christians to the energetic, still forthright, but now kindly and caring Christian apologist and pastor, it is contained in a single sentence: 'Let your conversation be always full of grace, seasoned with salt, so that you may know how to answer everyone.'[65]

The Greek New Testament word for grace is *charis*, from which we get 'charismatic'. In modern use it may describe a vivacious achiever, or a lively church. That risks losing the underlying sense of self-giving love. Grace is pre-eminently a quality of God. It is his gracious love poured on undeserving people through the life, death and resurrection of Jesus. 'It is by grace you have been saved, through faith,' says Paul.[66]

Grace is not a bland quality. It is full of energy and goodness. It is a rough equivalent of an Old Testament Hebrew word that is sometimes translated as 'loving-kindness', a term coined by the early English Bible translator Miles Coverdale. It has the idea of mutual respect between people who are bound together in an agreement or covenant. 'I have loved you with an everlasting love; I have drawn you with loving-kindness' was God's reassurance through Jeremiah to Judeans who felt that God had abandoned them.[67]

We are to reflect God's loving-kindness in what we say and do. It is how we conduct ourselves in public in order to commend Christ to others. Says commentator Tom Wright, 'Eagerness for witness must not be an excuse for harsh arrogance or boring complacency … Christians are to work at making their witness interesting, lively and colourful,' showing love and respect.[68]

Speech is to be 'seasoned with salt'. Salt was a precious commodity in the ancient world, in contrast to its overuse in processed foods today. Food in biblical times was bland unless it was seasoned, and imported spices were expensive. As well as a flavour enhancer, salt was a preservative; fish caught in Galilee would be salted for transport to markets in Jerusalem. If available in sufficient quantities, salt could also be used as a fertiliser, and still is in some places today.

Jesus referred to his followers as 'the salt of the earth'.[69] He expected them to put spiritual flavour, colour and life back into society. Through their good actions they would inhibit the rot that might otherwise set in and instead help to make the world a better place.

As western society seems to grow yet more loud, impatient, divided and anxious, it is more important than ever to recapture the virtues Paul described as 'the fruit of the Spirit': 'love, joy, peace, forbearance, kindness, goodness, faithfulness, gentleness and self-control'.[70] Two are especially neglected.

Act kindly and mercifully

The Greek word rendered 'kindness' is used more often of God than of people. That tells us that it reflects God's character in human relationships. It is related to forgiveness, and to mature, mellow wine.[71] So a kind person is a forgiving person, 'free from acidity and harshness', as the *Shorter Oxford English Dictionary* defines a mellow wine.

American Professor of Theology Lewis Smedes described kindness in language not usually associated with academics: 'Kindness is the will to save; it is God's awesome power channelled into gentle healing. Kindness is love acting on persons. Such kindness may be soft; it is not weak; tender but not feeble; sensitive, but not fragile.'[72] If you want to start meditating as part of your spiritual development, you could do worse than spend a week on those phrases.

Mercy is a related characteristic, and, like kindness, embraces the idea of compassion. God is described as 'merciful and gracious, slow to anger, and abounding in steadfast love and faithfulness'. In their debates, Jesus said the Pharisees were so preoccupied with tithing herbs that they neglected what he called 'the more important matters of the law – justice, mercy and faithfulness'.[73]

When he was criticised for eating with the common people, or for healing someone on the Sabbath, Jesus quoted the Old Testament and said, 'Go and learn what this means: "I desire mercy, not sacrifice."' The apostles spell out what mercy looks like in practice. James writes about looking after vulnerable people, supporting poor people, loving your neighbour whoever he or she is. He warns, 'judgment without mercy will be shown to anyone who has not been merciful'.[74]

Pope Francis declared 2016 to be a Year of Mercy, as the European refugee crisis hit its peak. The idea echoed the Old Testament principle of the Jubilee year, when Israelites were supposed to release slaves and return property to its original owners. It was a chance to start again and right some of the wrongs that may have been committed. The Pope wanted to encourage a spirit of welcome and compassion. Mercy is an action, not a feeling. 'Mercy does not mean not being cruel or sparing people revenge or punishment,' wrote Catholic journalist G. K. Chesterton; 'it means a plain and positive thing like the sun, which one has either seen or not seen.'[75]

Kindness and mercy: these are examples of love in action. 'Love is power and … kindness is the work of that power,' wrote Lewis Smedes. 'Kindness is the power that moves us to support and heal someone who offers nothing in return. Kindness is the power to move a self-centred ego toward the weak, the ugly, the hurt, and to move that ego to invest itself in personal care with no expectation of reward.'[76] Kindly love is powerful. It needs to be exercised with gentleness.

Handle gently

People are fragile. How many times we have noticed this in previous chapters! We are to handle one another with care. Gentleness is also a positive value, not a passive feeling. Several words are translated 'gentleness', each with different nuances, and one was rendered by Matthew Arnold, a nineteenth-century poet, as 'sweet-reasonableness'.

'It is an eminently sane quality,' wrote A. T. Schofield, a Christian Harley Street psychiatrist at the end of the nineteenth century. 'The better balanced a man is, the wiser, the more sure of himself, the gentler does he become, the more reasonable in his bearing to all. To me this sweet reasonableness of Christianity is a most precious and fragrant quality ... it is like an oasis in the desert to come across a spirit graced with it.'[77]

A gentle person is balanced and wise. Another biblical word for gentleness is sometimes translated as 'meekness'. That is unfortunate, given the image it may evoke. Biblically, the meek person is not a shrinking violet hiding away from others, nor a wallflower at the school prom afraid to ask someone to dance. 'Meekness' is the controlled strength of a trained animal. Think of a working dog, herding sheep to precise instructions, or a racehorse timing its jumps to perfection under the guidance of its jockey. Meekness is strength channelled into a positive and creative action. It is courage in the face of danger. It is restraint in the face of disappointment, and it is wisdom in the face of provocation.

The meek or gentle person is strong because they are trained by and obedient to God. Consequently, such a person 'acts with due consideration for the feelings of others, tempers justice with mercy and does not always insist on his rights'.[78]

The end is the beginning

Stop, listen, be thankful. Speak graciously, act kindly, handle gently. These are some of the potential outworkings of a transformed Christian mind. They are virtues which could make a big difference to our small corner of God's world – if, that is, we are willing to stand against the prevailing culture and embrace them.

If faith expressed like this sounds rather limp – fine in theory but hardly practical for a harsh and busy world – then listen to the view of Sir Ranulph Fiennes, the explorer and adventurer. According to a newspaper interview, he said that 'while recruiting members for a polar expedition he and his former exploring partner Charlie Burton discovered that the best candidates professed to have a deep faith'. In extreme circumstances, religion can give people a sense of purpose, he claimed, and admitted that 'faith helped him to deal with the threat of wanting to give up'.[79] The lives of such people, and those of their colleagues, depend on not messing up as they pursue difficult goals.

Christian faith can nurture strong character. The prophet Daniel declared, 'The people that do know their God shall be strong, and do exploits.'[80] They are equipped to avoid the Judas traps.

The ground we've covered in this chapter is broad. We really need to see how it might work in practice in the wider world. Among normal people who suddenly do abnormal things. Among people who are ostracised or who feel they are outsiders. Among people who are driven by obsessions. Among people who struggle with choices and feel they can't help themselves. Among people who have wealth, and among those who have none. Among people who find life more difficult than they can bear. Among people who love to gossip and to troll.

If that seems familiar, go back to where we started!

But whatever you do next, pause for thought first.

> Love is patient, love is kind. It does not envy, it does not boast, it is not proud. It does not dishonour others, it is not self-seeking, it is not easily angered, it keeps no record of wrongs. Love does not delight in evil but rejoices with the truth. It always protects,

always trusts, always hopes, always perseveres.
Love never fails.[81]

He has shown you, O mortal, what is good.
And what does the Lord require of you?
To act justly and to love mercy
and to walk humbly with you God.[82]

Notes

[1] Cited by Edward Jay Epstein, *Deception*, W. H. Allen, 1989, p.163; the origin of the saying is disputed.

[2] Christopher Andrew, *The Defence of the Realm*, Allen Lane, 2009, p.720.

[3] Frederic W. Farrar, *The Life of Christ*, Cassell and Co., 1898, pp.528-529.

[4] Colossians 1:16.

[5] Colossians 1:17; Hebrews 1:3; Isaiah 40:12-31; Matthew 10:29.

[6] See John 5:24-27; Acts 17:29-31; 2 Timothy 4:1; 2 Peter 3:9. The story of the prodigal son is in Luke 15:11-32.

[7] Romans 12:3.

[8] Romans 3:23-24.

[9] Stephen Fry, *The Fry Chronicles*, Michael Joseph, 2010, p.89.

[10] Psalm 51:5.

[11] 1 Timothy 4:2; Titus 1:15.

[12] Orlando Figes, *The Whisperers*, Penguin Books, 2008, pp.33-34.

[13] 1 Corinthians 4:4.

[14] 1 Corinthians 10:23–11:1.

[15] 'The truth hurts', *PR Week*, 2nd March 2007.

[16] *i*, 25th January 2012.

[17] Dorothy Rowe, *Why We Lie*, Fourth Estate, 2010, pp.50, 193.

[18] John 14:6, 26; 15:26; 16:7-11.

[19] John 8:32.

[20] William Barclay, *The Gospel According to John, Volume 2*, The St Andrew Press, 1965, p.25.

[21] Ephesians 4:25; Zechariah 8:16-17.

[22] Dorothy Rowe, *op. cit.,* p.298.

[23] Jonathan Aitken, *Pride and Perjury,* HarperCollins, 2000, p.69.

[24] John 18:38.

[25] Acts 17:27.

[26] Hebrews 1:1-2.

[27] Romans 5:7-8.

[28] Mark 12:29-31.

[29] Matthew 23:8-12; 1 Corinthians 12:12-13, 25.

[30] George Orwell, *Animal Farm,* Penguin Books, 1989 edition, pp.88, 90.

[31] Genesis 1:28.

[32] Acts 11:27-30; this visit may be the one referred to in Galatians 2:1-10.

[33] 2 Corinthians 8–9; Philippians 4:10-20.

[34] Matthew 28:19-20.

[35] Vincent Donovan, *Christianity Rediscovered,* SCM Press, 1982, pp.52-53.

[36] John 4:1-30; Matthew 15:21-28; Luke 7:1-10; Acts 1:8.

[37] Acts 15:1-35; Galatians 3:28-29.

[38] Luke 13:34-35; 19:41-44.

[39] Exodus 3:14.

[40] John 8:58-59; 10:31-39.

[41] Revelation 22:5; Psalm 90:4; 2 Peter 3:8.

[42] Ephesians 5:15-16.

[43] 2 Timothy 4:7-8.

[44] John 3:16.

[45] Romans 12:1-2 (as rendered by J. B Phillips, *The New Testament in Modern English,* Geoffrey Bles 1960; italics mine).

[46] 2 Corinthians 1:22, 5:17; John 3:3-8; Titus 3:5; 1 Peter 1:3.

[47] Philippians 2:12-13.

[48] Colossians 3:5-10.

[49] Robert Wicks, *Prayerfulness,* Sorin Books, 2009, p.34.

[50] Mark Williams and Danny Penman, *Mindfulness,* Piatkus, 2011, p.68.

[51] C. S. Lewis, *The Screwtape Letters,* Geoffrey Bles, 1961, p.101.

[52] C. S. Lewis, *Voyage to Venus,* Pan Books edition, 1953, p.128.

[53] Mark 9:7.

[54] Paul Tournier, *Escape from Loneliness,* SCM Press, 1967, pp.172-3.

[55] Martin Laird, *Into the Silent Land,* Darton Longman & Todd, 2006, pp.60-61.

[56] James 1:19.

[57] Proverbs 17:28.

[58] 2 Corinthians 12:20.

[59] Matthew 18:15-17.

[60] Daniel Defoe, *Robinson Crusoe*, Penguin Books, 1965, p.141.

[61] Luke 17:11-19.

[62] William Temple, *Readings in St John's Gospel*, Macmillan, 1945, pp.189-190.

[63] G. K. Chesterton, *A Short History of England*, Chatto & Windus, 1930, p.59.

[64] Philippians 4:6-7.

[65] Colossians 4:6.

[66] Ephesians 2:8.

[67] Jeremiah 31:3 (NIV 1984).

[68] N. T. Wright, *Colossians and Philemon*, InterVarsity Press, 1986, pp.153-154.

[69] Matthew 5:13.

[70] Galatians 5:22-23.

[71] Ephesians 4:32; Luke 5:39.

[72] Lewis Smedes, *Love Within Limits*, Lion Publishing, 1979, p.19.

[73] Exodus 34:6, *New Revised Standard Version*; Matthew 23:23.

[74] Matthew 9:13; 12:7; James 2:13.

[75] G. K. Chesterton, *Tremendous Trifles*, Methuen & Co., 1930, p.5.

[76] Lewis Smedes, *op. cit.*, pp.19-20.

[77] A. T. Schofield, *Christian Sanity*, revised and edited by J. Stafford Wright, Oliphants, 1965, p.28.

[78] Stephen Winward, *Fruit of the Spirit*, InterVarsity Press, 1981, p.178.

[79] *The Times*, 3rd October 2015.

[80] Daniel 11:32 (King James Version).

[81] 1 Corinthians 13:4-8.

[82] Micah 6:8.